The Perennial Philosophy

Series

World Wisdom
The Library of Perennial Philosophy

The Library of Perennial Philosophy is dedicated to the exposition of the timeless Truth underlying the diverse religions. This Truth, often referred to as the *Sophia Perennis*—or Perennial Wisdom—finds its expression in the revealed Scriptures as well as the writings of the great sages and the artistic creations of the traditional worlds.

Remembering in a World of Forgetting: Thoughts on Tradition and Postmodernism appears as one of our selections in the Perennial Philosophy series.

The Perennial Philosophy Series

In the beginning of the twentieth century, a school of thought arose which has focused on the enunciation and explanation of the Perennial Philosophy. Deeply rooted in the sense of the sacred, the writings of its leading exponents establish an indispensable foundation for understanding the timeless Truth and spiritual practices which live in the heart of all religions. Some of these titles are companion volumes to the Treasures of the World's Religions series, which allows a comparison of the writings of the great sages of the past with the perennialist authors of our time.

Cover: Stylized Celtic Eagle, from the Book of Dimma, an 8th century manuscript of the Gospels, Trinity College, Dublin

REMEMBERING IN A WORLD OF FORGETTING

Thoughts on Tradition and Postmodernism

by

William Stoddart

Edited by

Mateus Soares de Azevedo and

Alberto Vasconcellos Queiroz

World Wisdom

Remembering in a World of Forgetting: Thoughts on Tradition and Postmodernism

Library of Congress Cataloging-in-Publication Data

Stoddart, William.
Remembering in a world of forgetting : thoughts on tradition and postmodernism / by William Stoddart ; edited by Mateus Soares de Azevedo and Alberto Vasconcellos Queiroz.
p. cm. -- (The library of perennial philosophy) (The perennial philosophy series)
Includes bibliographical references and indexes.
ISBN 978-1-933316-46-8 (pbk. : alk. paper) 1. Postmodernism--Religious aspects. 2. Tradition (Theology) 3. Mysticism. I. Azevedo, Mateus Soares de, 1959- II. Vasconcellos Queiroz, Alberto, 1963- III. Title.
BL65.P73S76 2008
204--dc22

2007035475

Printed on acid-free paper in Canada.

For information address World Wisdom, Inc.
P.O. Box 2682, Bloomington, Indiana 47402-2682

www.worldwisdom.com

Other Works by the Same Author:

Hinduism and its Spiritual Masters
Outline of Buddhism
Sufism: The Mystical Doctrines and Methods of Islam

Books Edited:

Mirror of the Intellect by Titus Burckhardt
The Essential Titus Burckhardt
Religion of the Heart (with S. H. Nasr)

Contributions to:

Ye Shall Know the Truth: Christianity and the Perennial Philosophy (edited by Mateus Soares de Azevedo)
The Unanimous Tradition (edited by Ranjit Fernando)
In Quest of the Sacred (edited by S. H. Nasr and Katherine O'Brien)
Every Branch in Me (edited by Barry McDonald)
Sufism: Love and Wisdom (edited by Jean-Louis Michon and Roger Gaetani)
The Underlying Religion (edited by Martin Lings and Clinton Minnaar)

CONTENTS

List of Black-and-White Illustrations

PREFACE

Dr. William Stoddart has written over the years several books and many articles dealing with religion, spirituality, philosophy, and the modern world. No less important, he has also kept up a constant and voluminous correspondence about these same subjects with many people from many countries.

The standpoint from which Stoddart writes is that of the perennial philosophy or *sophia perennis*, whose main exponents in the last century were René Guénon, Ananda Coomaraswamy, Titus Burckhardt and, towering above them all, Frithjof Schuon. An idea as to what the perennial philosophy is, the reader will acquire, precisely, by reading this book.

Stoddart has devoted all his life to understanding this philosophy, and to living in accordance with it.

It is certainly as a result of this that, in his writings—books, essays, and letters—we find three very important characteristics: precision, simplicity, and essentiality.

Precision, one has to say, because Stoddart understands. He does not write about what he does not know, or knows only partially or superficially. He is not "discussing ideas", but expounding truths, be they concepts or facts. He knows that imprecision is contrary to Truth.

Simplicity, because he writes to help others to learn, and he knows—both in principle and from experience—that simplicity is the key to learning. He knows also that Truth is simple.

Essentiality, because he realizes that, to really understand religion, spirituality, and the perennial philosophy—and, on this basis, to understand the errors of the modern world—it is necessary to go to the essence of things, and not let oneself be dispersed in their multiple manifestations. He knows that it is always in the essential that we can find the true.

In this book, the reader will be sure to find the same characteristics. In a precise, simple, and essential way, it will help him to remember the most important truths—those which uncover the highest, and at the same time, the deepest meaning of man—and to apply them to the many aspects of human life.

It will also help him to realize concretely how important it is to practice this remembrance in a world which, precisely in relation to these truths, can certainly be defined as a world of forgetting.

Last but not least, Stoddart's book will help the reader to realize that precision, simplicity, and essentiality are fundamental keys for understanding and practicing this remembrance. It may also encourage him, like Stoddart himself, to devote his life to it.

Alberto Vasconcellos Queiroz

INTRODUCTION

The didactic exposition and explanation of traditional and universal *philosophy* (always in the sense of "love of wisdom") on the one hand, and the existential responsibility of man in relation to this perennial truth on the other: these are the twin poles between which revolve the axis of William Stoddart's writings.

In this book, Stoddart confronts the fact that the truth about God (the Absolute), man (the relative, or "lesser absolute"), and salvation (the "bridge" which the Absolute opens to the relative) has been almost totally forgotten. In other words, the world we live in is an "ambience of forgetfulness". What is needed therefore is "remembering".

But remembering what, and how?

Remembering first of all those truths that make human beings integrally men and women, truths which, as Frithjof Schuon said, are inscribed in the very substance of our being, but which have been covered over by many layers of confusion and forgetfulness.

And why have these truths been forgotten? First, because the very nature of our modern, so-called civilized world is forgetfulness of the True, the Good, and the Beautiful—to speak in the terms of Plato. It is now the "cult" of superficiality and mundanity that predominates. Because "civilization" has chosen to be interested only in what fades away, and not in what is everlasting; because it is busy with material and visible things, and not with the invisible and permanent things of the Spirit. Our natural intuition for the Sacred has been blunted by materialism and relativism.

In response, William Stoddart tells us that we should wake up and "remember". He shows that we have something to do about this situation, that we have a responsibility. And this is, first, to remember those truths which are inscribed in our hearts. And, second, to act in accordance with them.

Not without good reason, this stimulating volume explains, with clarity and concision, those fundamental dimensions of truth which are religion, orthodoxy, and mysticism.

Religion is, essentially, *religare*: to "re-link" or re-connect man to the Truth that transcends him, and which at the same time inhabits his most inward being. "God is nearer to us than our jugular vein", says an ancient Oriental tradition.

As far as orthodoxy is concerned, despite the many prejudices and the disinformation with which this concept is fraught, it simply means the correct manner, intellectually speaking, of understanding and actualizing the "link" just referred to. As Stoddart says, orthodoxy in the original Greek means "correct theory", and indicates the primacy of Truth over everything else. It is highly meaningful that the first step of the "Noble Eightfold Path" of the Buddha is precisely "correct opinion", namely "orthodoxy".

Stoddart speaks much of "tradition", in a rather special sense of this word. In the terminology of the perennial philosophy—the school of thought to which our author adheres—tradition means the continuity, and the projection to all aspects of life, of that which is originally made known to man by religious revelation. Tradition, in this sense, thus signifies extending the spiritual principles and values of religion to all dimensions of life, in different epochs, places, and peoples. It includes beliefs and practices, morality, social organization, the arts, comportment, and even the vestments of a given civilization. In this sense, tradition is the permeation of the whole of society by the values of the religion concerned.

After expounding and developing these central ideas of religion, orthodoxy, and tradition, Stoddart turns his attention, in the third part of the book, to "what we have to do", which he deals with under the heading of "spirituality". Here, the first subject is mysticism, which is nothing other than the profundity and sincerity of this re-connecting of man to the Absolute, the Absolute which, in this sense, is simply another name for transcendent Truth.

Stoddart's books and essays have been acclaimed for their clarity and accuracy. One reviewer wrote, in the North-American journal *Sophia* (4, 2, Winter 1998): "Stoddart has a tremendous capacity for synthesis; he is in fact a master of synthesis, an author who is able to extract the essence of the phenomena that he examines."

These same qualities are also present in this book. The reader has only to peruse his stimulating essays on spiritual figures from diverse civilizations, such as the Jagadguru of Kanchipuram, the great *jnânin* of 20th century India, and the contemplatives of Mount Athos in Greece, a center of Christian "remembrance" since the Middle Ages, to taste the flavor of mysticism.

We must also draw the attention of the reader to Stoddart's stimulating and profound treatment of capital topics such as Islamic spirituality and Buddhist Tantra. Not forgetting his discerning view on such contemporary topics as ethnic and religious conflict. His critique of the evolutionist hypothesis, his discussion of the ideological obstacles to the spiritual life, and of the importance of culture in education make this volume a rich field in which to delve in order to taste the intellectually nutritive and savory fruits of knowledge and understanding amid the sterile fields of modern and postmodern ideologies.

Indeed, the title and subtitle of this book, taken together, immediately provide us with two short but highly workmanlike definitions: Tradition is "remembering" and postmodernism is "forgetting". It could hardly be put more precisely!

There are many more original and stimulating chapters in *Remembering in a World of Forgetting* to which we would like to draw the reader's attention, but we would rather stop at this point. Enough has already been said to make it clear that William Stoddart writes for the intelligent reader, and he or she will certainly know the best way to find, in this rich treasure, the items that will interest him or her most. All that now remains for the editors is to say: "good reading"!

Mateus Soares de Azevedo

EDITORS' NOTE

We take pleasure in presenting to readers this compilation of William Stoddart's principal writings. Inevitably, in their original form, these contained a number of repetitions, most of which we have removed. Some, however, we have retained—in particular a few of the more important explanatory tables or diagrams—because we considered that these were essential to the chapter concerned, and that it would be a convenience for readers if we left them in place.

I.

Forgetting

"They reckon ill who leave Me out"

Ralph Waldo Emerson
(from his poem "*Brahma*")

1. PROGRESS OR THE "*KALI-YUGA*"?

Everywhere in the world today, men's aspirations are directed towards what is known as "progress". Though insuperable international dissensions and cruel regional wars have sown anxiety in the heart of man, they have not come near to shaking his belief that "man is progressing" and that "man must progress". That this should be so, in spite of world cataclysms, is not entirely surprising. Progress is looked on by most as being a matter of liberating the oppressed, feeding the hungry, healing the sick—and it is not strange that men should believe that anyone who might appear to oppose such endeavors must necessarily be a knave. Progress, however, is far from simply being age-old charity in modern dress; and while ideologists unremittingly expound the gospel of progress in all its myriad forms, many "simple" people know in their hearts that something has gone wrong.

But what is it that has gone wrong? If a man has a fever, who would deny him penicillin? If a man has a tumor, who would deny him surgery? But these questions by no means exhaust all aspects of the matter. There are not only antibiotics and anesthetics: there are also nuclear weapons and totalitarian oppressions.[1] All are the products of modern science, and all are the results of progress. Not even the most committed ideologist can separate the "good" effects from the "bad" and convince us that the former alone are progress, whereas the latter are not. The advances of scientific progress are "advances" which simply do not take man's comforts, wishes—or deepest needs—into account. Medicine and bombs, optimism and *Angst*, apparent freedom and real tyranny, are indissociable; the "good" and the "bad" aspects are thrown up *together*, willy-nilly. It is intellectual dishonesty to allege that man has it in his power to choose only the "good" effects and to reject the "bad", and it is self-deception to believe, against all probability, that the "good" effects will some day, somehow, outnumber the "bad".

[1] Characterized by universal thought-control by modern mass media (originally radio, and now television); technological surveillance (together with ruthless intimidation); mechanized weaponry (not swords or bows-and-arrows, but chemical and bacteriological warfare and machines of death). The least that can be said is that, qualitatively, the modern totalitarianisms are completely different from the ancient empires.

What is it then that has gone wrong? A hint is provided by the fact that progress, everywhere and always, is exclusively *material* progress. Contemporary reality is there to prove that collective "moral progress" is a cruel joke. In spite of organized schemes for social betterment, never has there been less virtue, less self-abnegation, less sanctity than today. It is true that in the world there are still some saints—more and more hidden, however, and alarmingly fewer than of old—but in any case what is decisive is that today neither the eyes of government nor of the masses are directed towards them. It is "clever" economists, false prophets, and populist politicians (be they "democratic" or "fundamentalist") who enjoy the limelight, and to use the word "virtue" in their regard is simply a mockery.

The gospel of "progress" rests on the belief that by means of natural sciences, intrinsically divorced from supernatural realities and revealed religion, man can improve the lot of his fellows. One might have hoped that more would see that this is a recipe which can only produce ever more numerous problems and drive human society deeper and deeper into turmoil. The worse our condition becomes, the more "science" is applied; the more "science" is applied, the worse our condition becomes. As the vicious circle turns, delinquency, anxiety, and discontent grow apace.

These words are not written in the belief that one day the majority of men will see the error of their "scientific" ways and, on taking thought, will set things right. Hindus understand why this cannot be so, for they know that we are living in the "Dark Age" (the *Kali-Yuga*),[2] and that the gravitational or "entropic" descent which we see everywhere around us and which stems from our blindness to supernatural reality, will continue inexorably till the cycle itself comes to its cataclysmic conclusion. This is the event which Christianity calls "the end of the world".

The clock cannot be turned back, and the world will continue its downward rush to its fearful doom. But whoever is capable of understanding the falseness of the progressivistic current around him, thereby liberates himself inwardly from the thraldom of a mortal error, even though outwardly he may not, any more than his fellows, escape its physical effects.

The Scriptures of all religions contain prophecies about the days when men will turn away from divine revelation and "Platonic" intuition alike, and put their faith instead in the shallow and shifting

[2] Indeed, the last phase of the *Kali-Yuga*!

notions invented by men. The Christian Gospel says: "It is impossible but that scandal will come"; and, lest anyone should regard the "scandal" with complacency, or even lend it his cooperation (as some woefully mistaken fundamentalists, rashly impatient for Armageddon, appear to do), it immediately adds: "but woe to him through whom scandal cometh"; those who are the agents of "progress" will not be held guiltless. In Islam, a counterblast to the doctrine of progress is to be found in the saying of the Prophet Mohammed: "No time cometh upon you but is followed by a worse." It is the opposite that is propagated by the media and taught in our schools. The Buddhist Scriptures and the traditions and prophecies of the Indians of North America likewise foresee man's collective falling away from religion, his ever increasing materialism in the latter days, and the fearful doom which lies ahead. But perhaps the most explicit intimation of the *Kali-Yuga* is to be found in the Scriptures of Hinduism. A well-known passage from the *Vishnu Purâna*, codified in the 3rd century A.D., reads like a description of the world around us and strikingly reveals the emptiness and hypocrisy of those who in the midst of increasing distress still talk about progress. For those with "eyes to see and ears to hear" this passage is a recall from illusion to reality and from falsehood to truth:

> Riches and piety will diminish daily, until the world will be completely corrupted. In those days it will be wealth which confers distinction, passion will be the sole reason for union between the sexes, and lies will be the only method for success in business. The earth will be valued only on account of the mineral treasures which it contains, disloyalty will be the means universally employed for continuing to exist, a simple ablution will be regarded as sufficient purification. . . .
>
> The observance of castes, laws, and institutions will no longer be in force in the Dark Age, and the ceremonies prescribed by the *Vedas* will be neglected. Women will obey only their whims and will be infatuated with pleasure. . . . Men of all kinds will presumptuously regard themselves as the equals of *brahmins*. . . . The *vaishyas* will abandon agriculture and commerce and will earn their living by servitude or by the exercise of mechanical professions. . . . The path of the *Vedas* having been abandoned, and man having been led astray from orthodoxy, iniquity will prevail and the length of human life will diminish in consequence. . . . Then men will cease worshiping Vishnu, the Lord of sacrifice, Creator and Lord of all things, and they will say: "Of what authority are the *Vedas*? Who are the Gods and the *brahmins*? What use is purification with water?. . ." The dominant caste will be that of *shûdras*. . . . Men, deprived of reason

and subject to every infirmity of body and mind, will daily commit sins: everything which is impure, vicious, and calculated to afflict the human race will make its appearance in the Dark Age.

2. MEANING BEHIND THE ABSURD

Space and time are the two fundamental conditions of our existence, but neither is unchanging, and this is particularly evident, as well as profoundly disturbing, to modern man.

For most of this century, it has been a commonplace to say that "the world is getting smaller". This has shown itself in two ways: modern communications on the one hand, and massive migrations on the other. These phenomena have given us the experience of having as "neighbors" peoples of whose very existence we may previously have been unaware. As a result of this, we now know concretely that, despite the seeming invincibility of modern uniformity (humanistic, skeptical, and amorphous), cultural plurality is still far from having been extinguished. It is notorious, however, that the foreign cultures and unfamiliar psychologies that now crowd in on us are in general badly understood. This is not helped by the fact that most cultures and psychologies—including both our own and the unfamiliar ones that cause us problems—have long since passed their prime, and frequently are no longer true to themselves, having assimilated, and been deformed by, many ugly modern poisons.

If "space" has unquestionably become smaller, "time" has unquestionably become more menacing. "Life is a dream" (*la vida es sueño*): Calderón's words remain true, but perhaps today they should be translated as "life is a nightmare", for this is exactly what life has become for vast numbers of people on our globe. Following the two world wars (affecting principally the "developed" countries), there have been, in all parts of the "third world", endless wars, revolutions, and repressions of the most cruel kind. This warfare (from 1914 onwards) is quite unprecedented, in the sense that in it modern science for the first time began, unmistakably and frighteningly, to reveal its true colors; as did, at the same time and equally frighteningly, the totally confused, bankrupt, and post-moral *Zeitgeist* or "spirit of the time". Both phenomena (and they are continuing and becoming worse) have been received by those who have most fully experienced them with inexpressible horror, incomprehension, and despair. They strike horror because, besides being evil, they are absurd.

If there is a universal truth, a perennial wisdom, a sacred science (as the ancient wisdom-systems, the world religions, and even the tribal cultures all combine to suggest), what bearing does this have, theoretically and practically, on the absurd anarchy and anarchic absurdity of these latter times? The received viewpoint is that traditional philosophies and religions are of historical and psychological interest only; but since (among other things) these ancient traditions can frequently be seen to combine homely wisdom and lofty subtlety, is it possible that they can be viewed alternatively as signposts to a deeper and more qualitative reality, of such a nature as might help to explain—and even counter—the manifestly superficial and quantitative state of absurdity which, in modern times, has made possible such unprecedented terror and despair throughout so many parts of the world?

Let there be no mistake about it: despite every setback, the received religion of our time is still an amalgam of evolutionism, progressivism, scientism, and psychologism. Unfortunately, the horrors resulting therefrom are dealt with simply by further doses of the same: and so the structures of society, and of "normalcy", are destroyed and consumed in an unending vicious spiral.

That the official religion is as described is proved by what happens if one shows any serious opposition to any of its elements: truly fundamental "heresy" of this kind provokes from the modernists a vituperation and vilification as savage and impassioned as anything that ever stemmed from religious bigotry in ages past. For the majority (who believe staunchly in the received religion) a business-like attack on evolutionism, progressivism, scientism, or psychologism is perceived as an attempt to fundamentally undermine their world, and they react with a corresponding violence and emotion.

In stark contrast to today's received religion are all the ancient religions (namely, Christianity, Islam, Buddhism, Hinduism, and native American religion) in their historic and pre-modern forms, in other words, in a pre-Freudian, pre-Marxist, and pre-Darwinist context. It is therefore of paramount importance to study the intellectual contents of these religions (and what these contents mean) and to explore how this meaning can be applied to the interpretation—and handling—of current cruelties and absurdities. Our approach to such a study must be, not experimental and empirical, but consciously "Platonic". And this bespeaks a "Platonism" which is explanatory, peace-giving, and saving.

The central intellectual characteristic of the specifically modern age is what one might call the "abolition of the Absolute". (That the resulting vacuum is subsequently filled with all sorts of false "absolutes" is another question).

The "false prophets" of the 19th and early 20th centuries (three of them—Freud, Marx, Darwin—have just been mentioned) are still very much with us, but they have been discussed to satiety for many decades. In any case, there are two other "false prophets", dominating the second half of the 20th century, who, far from being seen in their true colors, are widely regarded as angels of light. I refer here to Carl Jung and Teilhard de Chardin. Freud is obviously pretty gross. Jung, to many, appears to be the friend of religion. For this very reason, the great spokesman of the "traditionalist" school, René Guénon, called Jung worse than Freud. In "Tradition and the Unconscious" (chapter 7 of *Fundamental Symbols: The Universal Language of Sacred Science*), Guénon says that Freud had "a clearly satanic character", but that this was nevertheless "still limited to a certain extent by his materialistic attitude". Referring to Jung, however, Guénon speaks of "false spirituality" and of a "much more subtle confusion".

Traditionally (i.e. according to Eckhart, Ibn 'Arabî, and other classical masters of gnosis), man is made up of three elements, namely Spirit (or Intellect), soul, and body. (*Please see the upper table on p. 46.*)

The Spirit, although "created" is supra-formal or universal, and directly touched by the Divine. It is the only supra-individual, "archetypal", or objective element in man's constitution. Spirit and Intellect are two sides of the same coin, the latter pertaining to Truth (or doctrine) and the former to Being (or spiritual realization). The soul, on the other hand, is formal and individual. The Spirit is therefore the "measure" of the soul; the soul can never be the "measure" of the Spirit. Jung's error, in a nutshell, is his complete confusion of Spirit and soul, which in practice amounts to an "abolition" of the Spirit.[1] This is the "abolition of the Absolute" with a vengeance!

As for the second "wolf in sheep's clothing", Teilhard de Chardin, his "ghost" may be said to have been the architect of the Second Vatican Council, and his is the most strident voice to date of the doctrines of materialism, evolutionism, and progressivism. Titus Burckhardt commented on his central thesis as follows:

[1] Amongst the soul's faculties are: mind (or reason), will, affect (or sentiment), imagination, and memory. (*Please see the lower table on p. 46.*) In everyday parlance, "Intellect" is often misleadingly used to signify mind or reason. In traditional metaphysics, it is correctly used in the transcendent sense in which (as indicated above) it is virtually synonymous with "Spirit". There is no impenetrable barrier between mind (or reason) and Intellect: the relationship of the latter to the former is like the relationship of the pinnacle of a cone to its circumferential base.

> Man possesses the capacity for objectivity, and it is on the basis of this that he makes judgements and assertions. If this capacity be no more than a phase in an on-going evolution—which, seen as a whole, is to be compared to a curve or a spiral—then this phase cannot step out of the whole and say: I am part of a spiral. Anything that such an evolution-bound faculty could conceive or express would also be subject to evolution. It would thus lack any absolute character, and this is why it is completely incapable of satisfying the basic logical requirements of a normal man.

It is because of the anti-Platonic, anti-Aristotelian, and anti-Thomistic character of the modern age, that one can say that its chief intellectual characteristic is the "abolition of the Absolute". Quite simply, it is an age of "nominalism", existentialism, and error, in which relativism and subjectivism run riot, with catastrophic results for both the individual and society. The only antidote to the relative and the subjective is the absolute and the objective, and it is precisely these that are the contents of traditional philosophy or "perennial wisdom" (*sophia perennis*) which says of itself: "From the beginning, and before the creation of the world, was I created, and unto the world to come, I shall not cease to be" (*Ecclesiasticus*, 24, 14). Using the term "esoterism" (seen as the "total truth") as synonymous for *sophia perennis*, Frithjof Schuon summarily rejects subjectivism and relativism, and describes man's true position, as follows:

> The prerogative of the human state is objectivity, the essential content of which is the Absolute. There is no *knowledge* without objectivity of the intelligence, no *freedom* without objectivity of the will, and no *nobility* without objectivity of the soul. Esoterism seeks to realize pure and direct objectivity; this is its reason for being.

Thus true "esoterism" is the only key to knowledge, freedom, and nobility; it is the only source of the objective and the absolute, and the only antidote to error. Esoterism, as understood here, is identical with traditional philosophy (i.e. Platonism, Thomism, or any other venerable wisdom-system). It is not the enemy of revealed religion, as those familiar only with the many contemporary pseudo-esoterisms have found reason to suppose. Schuon continues: "Just as rationalism can remove faith, so esoterism can restore it."

Faced with an already centuries-old deviation from absolute and objective truths and values, mocked and threatened by the shallowness, ugliness, cruelty, and absurdity of so much of the modern world, a deep study of the belief systems and wisdom-systems of the past offers us a solid way of hope, reassurance, and release.

3. TRADITIONAL AND MODERN CIVILIZATIONS

T. S. Eliot wrote that each of the great world cultures—Byzantine, Medieval, Islamic, Chinese, or other—is the social and artistic expression of a religious revelation. Each revelation is handed down—unchanged in essence but increasingly elaborated in expression—by the power of tradition. It is through this social and artistic deployment which we call "tradition" that the original revelation comes to permeate, and imprint its particular stamp on, every sector of collective life; and it is precisely this permeation of society by religion that enables us to speak of a "traditional" civilization.

Modern civilization, on the contrary, is the only civilization in history that was not founded on religion. In its origin, and in its subsequent unfolding, it is entirely secular and humanist. It had its first stirrings in the 14th century, at the tail-end of the Middle Ages, and came into full spate with the 15th-century "Renaissance" and the 18th-century "Enlightenment". It has developed at an ever-increasing pace right up to our own day: both the first half and the second half of the 20th century have provided us with a surfeit of unsavory examples of the nature and characteristics of modern "civilization".

I venture to add, without any euphemism, that, for the fully-fledged "traditionalist", these great cultural cataclysms—the "Renaissance" and the "Enlightenment"—have nothing to do with "re-birth" or "light"! On the contrary, they are seen, not as advances, but as successive impoverishments! It is for precisely this reason that the traditionalists see a perfect religious and cultural equivalence between Medieval Christian civilization (the age of the cathedrals, the age of the illuminated Gospel manusscripts, the age of faith) and the religious civilizations of the East. All of these traditional civilizations are to be contrasted with the post-Renaissance, post-Enlightenment, and post-Industrial-Revolution civilization of today. I do not think that this analysis is controversial. What is controversial is the value judgement which we make with regard to the two opposing sets of principles. For it is not a question of a gradual historical process. The Renaissance, and its repetition in the form of the Enlightenment, were conscious revolutionary breaks with the traditional past. It was with these breaks—seen as advances by some and impoverishments by others—that Europe became different from the rest of the world. That there are two opposing sets of principles—the traditional and the modern—is precisely what is elucidated with such clarity and authority in the works of the authors of the "traditionalist" or "perennialist" school. (*See chapter 11 for a full discussion of this school.*)

In considering here the contrast between traditional and modern civilizations, we will have recourse to Titus Burckhardt's analysis of this in his book *Fez, City of Islam.* As a young man, in the nineteen-thirties, Burckhardt spent some years in Morocco, where he established intimate friendships with some remarkable representatives of the as yet intact heritage of the Islamic Far-West. Already at the time concerned, he committed much of his experience to writing. Not all of this was immediately published, and it was only much later that his definitive works appeared.

In his book on Fez, Burckhardt relates the history of a people and its religion—a history that was often violent, often heroic, and sometimes holy. Throughout the book Burckhardt traces the thread of traditional Islamic mores and attitudes, and he uses these to introduce us to the meaning of the traditional way of life as such. He helps us to understand not only, let us say, remote Tibet or remote Tamilnad, but also our own European Middle Ages—for example the Celto-Christian world of Kells, Iona, and Lindisfarne, and the Saxon and Norman periods in England.

Basing himself on the city of Fez, Burckhardt conveys many of the teachings, parables, and miracles of the Maghribi sages and saints of many centuries, and demonstrates not only the arts and crafts of Islamic civilization, but also its "Aristotelian" sciences and its administrative skills. There is much to be learnt about the governance of men and of nations from Burckhardt's presentation of the principles lying behind dynastic and tribal vicissitudes—with their failures and their successes. His book is rich in historical clarifications, artistic appreciations, and philosophical insights.

The chapter on "Traditional Science" is an open window onto the subtleties and insights of pre-humanist, or "Aristotelian", thinking. Most people (except, no doubt, people like C. S. Lewis) are quite unaware of the breadth and depth of pre-modern thinking. Some may have familiarity with ancient Greek philosophy, but here, in the examples given in Burckhardt's book, we see the same ancient attitudes still, as it were, in operation.

The chapter entitled "The Golden Chain" is a poetic evocation of Sufism or Islamic mysticism. Burckhardt stresses that, in Sufism, the two classical spiritual "ways"—of "knowledge" and of "love"—together constitute the path towards God and salvation, which is the *raison d'être* of human life.

What relevance can the writings (be they historical or spiritual) of the traditionalists have for us today? Well, they do provide insights into one or two contemporary problems. It could perhaps be said that two of the greatest evils of the age are atheism on the one hand and religious "fundamentalism" on the other. Atheism in its brutal communist mode has already foundered, but of course it continues in other ways. "Fundamentalism" or "communalism" (an Anglo-Indian term derived from the expression ethnic or "communal" conflict) is now rampant world-wide and is forcibly brought to our attention every day. This all too prevalent disease of our times is discussed in detail in a later chapter entitled "Religious and Ethnic Conflict". The study of traditional civilizations opens our eyes to a world in which the prevailing state of soul was, to a significant extent, the exact opposite to what has just been described. Traditional religion and piety, by definition, gave priority to the Inward, not the outward. True, man was still man, and there were crusades, holy wars, and *jihâds*—though one has to say that the religious civilizations which they were allegedly fighting for were still religious. However, both the hagiography and the arts of the traditional periods prove beyond doubt that it was the Inward—or the spiritual—that predominated in the mind and soul of the people. The appellation "age of faith" was not awarded by the historians for nothing.

The overriding benefit, for the contemporary world, of "traditionalist" writings such as those of Burckhardt is their ability to make clear that the essential is to see beyond the form to the content, and, within the content of the various religions and cultures, to discern the supra-formal Truth and saving Way. "Supra-formality" of this kind is possible only on the basis of respecting, and understanding in depth, the meaning and function of the various revealed forms, which in reality are but different languages and pathways of the one Divine Message.

4. IDEOLOGICAL OBSTACLES TO THE SPIRITUAL LIFE

"That which is 'below' cannot worship that which is 'above', if that which is 'left' does not honor that which is 'right'. Our relationship with God includes our relationship with God's reflection on the earthly plane" (Frithjof Schuon). In other words, our "vertical" relationship with God (prayer, remembrance) is impaired to the extent that our "horizontal" relationship with God's reflections on earth (truth, justice, virtue, beauty) is insufficient.

Lack of discrimination (mental acuity) and lack of imagination in fallen man ensure that imperfections in the "horizontal" relationship are commonplace. For example, one should not have wrong views on such a thing as politics. One must either, in a genuinely dispassionate and non-bitter manner, remain totally detached from having a political opinion or, alternatively, one must have right views! These views (apart from being based on sufficient information) must be "traditional" and "conservative"—but not of course in a political party sense. Not everyone has the possibility of acquiring sufficient information and, when this is the case, one must either completely abstain from having a political opinion, or else develop a sound intuition or "instinct" for what is right. This is easier said than done, on the one hand, because habit, poor imagination, insufficient information, mental lethargy and unconscious passion paralyze objective thinking (resulting, most commonly, in flagrant "double standards") and, on the other, because our upbringing inevitably took place not merely in an ambience of "democracy", but in the presence of the ideas of *marxism*, *psychoanalysis*, and *evolutionism* (or *progressivism*), and it is more difficult to escape from the pervasive influence of these ideas than one might think. Furthermore, because of "poor thinking" (due to the causes just mentioned), there is also the possibility of an unhealthy reaction to these modern ideas *par en bas* ("by the downward path"). This indeed is the case of the various contemporary "fundamentalisms".

Not in practical political terms, but ideally, and in the last analysis, conservatism is "inwardness" (or depth) and socialism is "outwardness" (or superficiality). It is the distinction between quality and quantity. The terms "conservatism" and "socialism" are used here merely as symbols for two opposing tendencies. It will easily be seen that, while today there is much "socialism" (and pseudo-conservatism), there is little "conservatism" in the true and traditional sense.

Furthermore, there exists, in the modern world, a plethora of overtly fallacious ideologies, the espousal of any one of which fatally impairs one's "vertical" relationship with God. For example, one cannot follow a spiritual way and at the same time be a humanist, a socialist, a feminist, a nationalist, a nazi, a communist, or a zionist. The motivating force behind all of these "-isms" is, on the one hand, an impulse towards innovation and experiment and, on the other, a desire for the security and feeling of strength that can be obtained from collectivism. They are above all vain searchings for solutions at a purely outward and superficial level.

It may be helpful to have recourse to the Hindu cosmological theory of the three *gunas* or "cosmic tendencies"; these are: *sattva* (the upward tendency), *rajas* (the expansive tendency), and *tamas* (the downward tendency). Using these terms one can say that "conservatism" is sattvic and "socialism" is tamasic. *Rajas* (the expansive tendency or "passion") can be allied to either one or the other. Let us briefly consider these "-isms" one by one:

Humanism is placing the Second Commandment (to love one's neighbor) before the First Commandment (to love God), and then to omit the First Commandment altogether. Fundamentally, it is to place man's ego (singular or collective) above God.

Socialism (a form of humanism) means putting our faith in a quantitative collectivity rather than in a qualitative principle. It is the natural without the supernatural.

Feminism means following "Eve" rather than "Mary". Eve was the one who said "the serpent told me to do it"; Mary was the one who "bruised the serpent's head with her heel". Following Eve (the "below") means listening to the sweet and seductive song of the sirens—which however ultimately leads to disaster and sorrow. Following Mary (the "above") means at first effort, with all the hardness and clarity of a diamond, but ultimately leads to liberation and joy. "I am black, but beautiful" (Song of Solomon, 1, 5). (*See also p. 67.*)

Nationalism—as Peter Townsend and others have pointed out—is collective egoism, and as such, it is no more beautiful than individual egoism. It is to derive vulgar pleasure from narcissism and xenophobia. Once again, one has to say that it is a stupidity as well as an evil. Linked with nationalism are "separatism" (to the extent that it is illegitimate), communalism, and "patriotism". As regards separatism: the so-called principle of "self-determination" is always debatable, and especially so when it is pushed to the extreme. "Communalism" is the British term for ethnic and/or denominational strife. Today it is ubiquitous, and worse than ever.

As regards patriotism: a naive and simple patriotism is natural to man. The man of the mountains loves mountains and mountain people. Those who live on the sea coasts are often fishermen: they love the dangerous and courageous life of sea-fishing, and they love the fisher folk. Today, however, what is called "patriotism" is all too frequently synonymous with nationalism, and there are few things more shaming. It should be obvious that it is illusory to think that one can or should have feelings of "patriotism" towards an immense secular (or falsely religious) and heterogeneous collectivity—a collectivity which, in any case (with its ubiquitous pornography, rock music, and drug taking), is fundamentally degenerate. The worst thing of all (and it is widespread) is the linking of this "patriotism" with religion: "God and country." It is completely overlooked that, in the Decalogue, Almighty God says: "Thou shalt have no other gods before Me." This also means: "Thou shalt not create gods who are equal to Me." "For the Lord thy God is a jealous God; Him only shalt thou serve." The Muslims say: "Thou shalt not 'associate' anything with Allah."

Nazism is humanism in Babylonian and draconian mode. It is a vain, vulgar, and violent striving after a greatness without God.

Communism is atheism—cruelly and systematically enforced. Its primary goal is the extirpation of religion. This is accompanied by the deadly hand of a centrally controlled economy. In the Russia (or rather the "USSR") of the 20s and 30s, the deliberately brutal implementation of this bureaucratic inefficiency led to the death of tens of thousands of people. There is a multitude of harrowing accounts of the religious persecution of Christianity (in the European sector) and of Islam (in the central Asian countries).

Zionism is the parody of a Biblical prophecy. It is communalism, materialism, and socialism. It is not a love of the Hebrew prophets, such as, for example:

Moses:	"Hear, O Israel, the Lord is our God, the Lord is one."
Esdras:	"Great is the Truth and it shall prevail."
Micah:	"What does the Lord require of thee, but to do justly, to love mercy, and to walk humbly with thy God."
David:	"The Lord is my shepherd, I shall not want."
Solomon:	"The fear of the Lord is the beginning of wisdom."

These great Prophets (all of whom prophesied or hinted at the coming of the Messiah) constitute Judaism. As traditional Jews have often pointed out, Zionism is a desacralization of the religion of Judaism. It is not religious, but secular.

In condemning secularism and extolling religion, it is nevertheless important to remember that what today is called "religion" is often the worst parody of all. Alas, I am not only thinking of the cults and the "new age"! The numerous pseudo-religious ideologies of today, rather misleadingly called "fundamentalisms" (and starting with "the religious right"—or at least a large portion thereof—in North America), are far indeed from the inspired teachings of the great Prophets, Christian or other. There are few, if any, purely "religious" political parties in the West, but there are quite a number in Asian and North African countries. The trouble with these "religious" parties is that they are not religious—quite the contrary! They invariably combine a superficial religious formalism with a modern psychology and an avid espousal of modern technology. To have a religion truly involves having a normal psychology and a modicum of spiritual intuition. For true religion implies depth, not surface. It is personal, and not *a priori* collective. It aims at salvation, not at a spirit-less—and in any case unrealizable—utopia. It is a typically modern paradox that, in several countries, political parties which call themselves "secular" are distinctly better than parties which claim for themselves the epithet "religious".

All of the modern "-isms" are characterized by stupidity, vulgarity, superficiality, and collectivism. Many have also involved massive cruelty—both according to the explicit words of their founders (Hitler and Lenin, for example) and in actual practice. In brief, all of the above "-isms" are modalities of the underlying lie of atheism. They represent the usurpation of quality by quantity, of profundity by superficiality, and finally of God by unregenerate man.

The spirit of the Vatican II Council of 1960-1965 is an ideology that is strictly analogous to the "-isms" castigated above; it is one that is hostile to all religion; and so are the "Islamic republic" of Khomeini in Iran and the "Islamic revolution" of Qadhâfî in Libya.

Nothing said above is intended to be an exoneration of industrialism (or industrialist capitalism), which also has its share of many of the negative characteristics mentioned.

*

* *

It is necessary also to mention the "ideology" of world-wide terrorism, for example, in Northern Ireland (Protestants against Catholics and vice versa), in former Yugoslavia (Orthodox against Catholics, and Orthodox against Muslims), in the Middle East (Muslim suicide bombers against Zionist settlers), in Sudan (Muslims against Muslims—also Muslims against Christians), in Iraq (Shi'is against Sunnis and vice versa), in Pakistan (Muslims against other Muslims for a variety of reasons), in the Punjab (Sikhs against Hindus), in Kashmir (Hindus against Muslims), in Sri Lanka (Hindus against Buddhists and vice versa), in Burma (Buddhists against Christians). And so on. Nothing could be further from the Will of God, and the way of the angels.

The essential evil of the terrorists is their claim to be carrying out their nefarious acts in the name of their religion. True, in many cases, there is an underlying injustice against which one may reasonably be indignant. But given the extreme evil of the terrorists' means, their claim to be acting in the name of God is the ultimate blasphemy. In such cases, the means gravely compromise the end. A defining characteristic of terrorists—one that is obvious, and yet often overlooked—is their self-granted "autonomy"; they are in most cases "irregulars", acting beyond the control of their respective government and community, and in disobedience to them. All of the above has the result that the terrorists fatally undermine the cause which they allegedly support.

*

*   *

The arrogant choice of, as it were, "Eve" rather than "Mary", of the shallow rather than the deep, of the false rather than the true, of the quantitative rather than the qualitative, of the "politically correct" rather than justice, of "new age" religion (easy) rather than authentic religion (hard)—and many other analogous choices—have contributed massively, in the last few decades and even in the last few years, to the accelerating descent of the world.

5. RELIGIOUS AND ETHNIC CONFLICT IN THE LIGHT OF THE WRITINGS OF THE PERENNIALIST SCHOOL

If one wished to sum up in one word the central evil of the modern age, one could do so with the word "atheism". While this diagnosis might command ready agreement on the part of religiously-minded people, it might still, because it seems too abstract or too general, be regarded as a trifle facile. Nevertheless, I believe that, in one or more of its many guises, it is precisely atheism that is at the root of all modern evils. Atheism may be as ancient as fallen man, but the atheism that is with us today has its direct origin in the ideas of the 18th century "Enlightenment"—the ideas espoused by Voltaire, Rousseau, and the *encylopédistes.*

Of course, I use the term "atheism" in an extremely comprehensive way, and I include in it things not usually perceived as being directly atheistic, such as illogic, unimaginativeness, indifference, and complacency—all so many denials of God (and thus so many abdications of humanity) without which such absurd but successful hoaxes as evolutionism, psychologism, and marxism would never have been possible.

In the 20th century, the most explicit and brutal form of atheism was Soviet communism. A few years ago, after seventy years of pretense and pretension during which it enjoyed the enthusiastic approval of "enlightened" academia—it foundered in a really big way. Needless to say, the evil and the ignorance that took concrete form in communism have not simply evaporated. They cannot but find other forms of expression.

When something is perceived as bad, there are usually reactions to it, and these in turn can be either good or bad. There was the reaction to worldliness of St. Francis of Assisi, a "second Christ" (*alter Christus*) who, through the strength of his faith and his asceticism, reanimated and reinvigorated the Christian tradition for centuries to come. One could perhaps think of other renewals of this kind, but such reactions to the bad are rare indeed. Nowadays, most reactions to what is perceived as evil are themselves evil: they are reactions, not *par en haut* ("by the upward path"), but *par en bas* ("by the downward path"). It is as if the devil took charge of the reactions against his own work—and used them to his further advantage.

Examples of bad reactions to atheism or secularism are not hard to find. In keeping with the age we live in, they are invariably forms of collectivism of one sort or another. Collectivism means the generation of quantitative power from below. Its opposite is spontaneous submission to qualitative power from above. This latter involves individual responsibility and the ability to recognize legitimate authority. In the past, people *submitted* to the self-evident truths of religion; today they espouse, in mass movements, the *outward trappings* of religion. Khomeinîism and Qadhâfiism are cases in point. So are Serbian and Hindu and many other contemporary nationalisms. This form of collectivism may be called "denominationalism".

Like other collectivisms, denominationalism is anything but eirenic; it is the direct source of a viciously aggressive competitiveness between religious and cultural communities, which is properly known as "communalism"—a term that was first used in this sense in India. Communalism, in the form of inter-religious conflict, has today become a world-wide epidemic. But do we know its exact nature? It is the rivalry, to the death, of two neighboring *religious* nationalisms. We are witnesses to the war between Azerbaijanis and Armenians, and to the war between Roman Catholic Croats and Eastern Orthodox Serbs. (Each of these rival ethnicities has contributed cruelly to the tragic destruction of largely Muslim Bosnia, and particularly the historic cities of Sarajevo and Mostar). In Sri Lanka the communal rivalry is between Buddhists and Hindus, in the Panjab between Hindus and Sikhs, in Ayodhyâ and elsewhere in India it is between Muslims and Hindus, in Cyprus between Greeks and Turks, and in Northern Ireland between Catholics and Protestants. Each grouping adheres to its denomination and its culture in a passionate but nevertheless superficial and formalistic way, and in a manner which lethally challenges a neighboring and equally superficial and formalistic cultural loyalty. These groupings are often called fundamentalist, but in their ideology they are invariably modern, progressivist, and collectivist. Communalism has been well described as "collective egoism". The last thing that one expects to find in these fanatical groupings is spirituality or piety. Not the Inward, but the outward in its most brutal and superficial mode, is their concern. They defend the form while killing the essence; they will kill for the husk, while trampling on the life-giving kernel. They kill not only their putative religious rival: they have already killed themselves. Communalism, like all shallow—but consuming—passion, is suicidal.

It might be said that one can find a prefiguration of communalism in the "holy wars" of ages past—the Crusades, for example—in which two traditional systems were pitted against one another, each one viewing the other as the representative of evil. It is a far cry, however, from the holy wars, chivalric or otherwise, of the Middle Ages to the mindless hatreds and mechanized exterminations of modern times.

There is no doubt, however, that the seismic "crack" or "fault" which runs through former Yugoslavia, Ukraine, and elsewhere in Eastern Europe does have its origin in an ancient division, namely, the "Great Schism" of A.D. 1054.[1] It is the dividing line between Eastern and Western Christendom. I doubt if there is any more bitterly-manned frontier in the whole world. This is a chilling reminder in the contemporary Western climate of facile and superficial ecumenism.

In view of the ancient origin of most of the present-day communal divisions, it could perhaps be objected that communalism is no more than the instinct of self-preservation, and that, as such, it is as old as mankind. However, this is far from being the case. For very many centuries, the world was divided into great empires, each comprising a variety of peoples and often a variety of religions. The Anglo-Greek traveler and author Marco Pallis once made mention of an 18th century Tibetan book which (from the standpoint of Tibet) referred to the four great empires, which to them seemed to encompass the world: the Chinese, the Mughal, the Russian, and the Roman. By this last term they meant Christendom or Europe.

It was at the end of World War I that several empires that had encompassed many different peoples and religions crumbled: the Prussian, the Austro-Hungarian, the Ottoman. Many new countries appeared: Poland, Czechoslovakia (now Czechia and Slovakia), Yugoslavia (now broken into seven parts), amongst others. Also several independent Arab countries emerged from the Ottoman Turkish empire. All this required an "ideological" basis, and this was found in 1918 in the "Fourteen Points" of President Woodrow Wilson, one

[1] The essential cause of the schism was the theological dispute regarding the procession of the Holy Spirit. The Eastern Church adhered to the original form of the early creeds which declared that the Holy Spirit proceeds from the Father; the Western Church, on the other hand, introduced the doctrine that the Holy Spirit proceeds from the Father *and from the Son* (in Latin, *Filioque*).

of which was "self-determination", the first time these fateful words achieved prominence. The idea may have been well-intentioned—a safeguard against putative imperial oppression—but it has since become a dogma of the modern world and of the United Nations, and is the "philosophical" justification of almost all current communalism and ethnic conflict. To paraphrase the words of the late Professor John Lodge, often quoted by Ananda Coomaraswamy: from the four great empires known to the Tibetans to the present-day "United Nations", *quelle dégringolade*!

*

* *

Let us leave communalism for a moment, and turn to a very different phenomenon of our times. This is what the American Academy of Religion has called "the perennialist or esoterist school", of which the founders were the French philosopher and orientalist René Guénon (1886-1951) and the German philosopher and poet Frithjof Schuon (1907-1998), and which was further expounded by Ananda Coomaraswamy (1877-1947) and Titus Burckhardt (1908-1984). This is discussed in full in a later chapter entitled "Frithjof Schuon and the Perennialist School", but we may note here that its principal characteristics include the fundamental and essential principles of metaphysics (with its cosmological and anthropological ramifications), intellectual intuition, orthodoxy, tradition, universality, the science of symbolism; spirituality in the broadest sense; intrinsic morals and esthetics; and the meaning and importance of sacred art. A very important characteristic is a deep-reaching critique of the modern world, on the basis of strictly traditional principles. Above all, like Pythagoras and Plato, Guénon and Schuon derive their doctrinal expositions directly from *intellectus purus*—a process which lends to these expositions an unsurpassable lucidity, not to say infallibility.

This supra-formal truth constitutes the *religio perennis*. This term, which does not imply a rejection of the similar terms *philosophia perennis* and *sophia perennis*, nevertheless contains a hint of an additional dimension which is unfailingly present in Schuon's writings. This is that intellectual understanding entails a spiritual responsibility, that intelligence requires to be complemented by sincerity and faith, and that "seeing" (in height) implies "believing" (in depth). In other words, the greater our perception of essential and saving truth, the greater our obligation towards an effort of inward or spiritual "realization".

I have called this perennialist current of intellectuality and spirituality "a phenomenon of our times"—but unlike other phenomena of today, it is a secret one, a "still small voice", a hidden presence, sought out and found only by those with a hunger and thirst for it, and known only to those with eyes to see and ears to hear.

*

* *

Returning to communalism: at the outward level, this is sometimes addressed in a desultory and piece-meal way by what is called "the international community". And of course, the United States has become embroiled in a war that is linked with this question. Inevitably, the response to such efforts is highly uneven—experience has shown that there is no one who can effectively "police" the entire world. Such sympathy as is extended to victims is on a humanitarian basis towards individuals. It does not comprehend or consider the value of communities, collectivities, or what we might call "traditional civilizations", be these ethnic or religious, and it is they which are at risk. It is precisely such religious communities—be they Tibetan Buddhists or Bosnian Muslims—that are in danger of being destroyed by a powerful (and sinisterly "idealistic") neighbor—something much less likely to happen when they were part of a large, but tolerant (because "realistic") empire. The Austro-Hungarian empire encompassed, ethnically speaking, Germans, Magyars, and Slavs and, religiously speaking, Roman Catholicism, Eastern Orthodoxy, and Islam. I have myself visited many mosques in Bosnia, and in several of them I saw magnificent Persian prayer carpets donated by the Emperor Franz Josef. This is a courtesy unlikely to be extended to the Slavic Muslims by the competing religious nationalism of their neighbors, whose sentiments, on the contrary, have shown themselves to be exterminatory! Both Frithjof Schuon and Titus Burckhardt have mentioned in their writings that kings and nobles often had a wisdom and a tolerance unknown in a denominationally-motivated clergy—today it would be known as an ideologically-motivated political élite—who unfortunately have it in their power to influence the people along denominationalist, or inanely ideological, lines. A similar point was made by Dante, who, for intellectual and spiritual reasons, sided with the Emperor, and not the Pope.

*

*   *

Communalism derives from denominationalism. Communalism is obviously outward; denominationalism, being an attitude of mind, could perhaps be described as "falsely inward". There is virtually nothing that we as individuals can do outwardly about communalism; but we can always keep under review our attitudes towards our own denomination, and be on guard against any slipping into what I have called "denominationalism" (which the French call "confessionalism"). We must not, even within ourselves, give comfort to communalism by consciously or unconsciously participating in the denominationalism that makes it possible.

As I have mentioned, the traditionalist writings are largely an exposition of the *religio perennis*, the "underlying religion" of essential truth and saving grace which is at the heart of each great revelation (and of which each great revelation is the providential "clothing" for a particular sector of humanity). Because of this relationship between the "underlying religion" and its various "providential clothings", it is necessary for anyone wishing access to this "underlying religion" to do so by espousing one particular traditional and orthodox religion, to believe and understand its central theses (its "dogmas"), and to participate in its way of sanctification (its "sacraments"). The universalism of the perennialist does not mean dispensing with sacred forms that were revealed by God for our salvation. There is no other way than through these. The perennialist is simply aware that the Formless must needs be represented on earth by a plurality of forms. The contrary is an impossibility.

To return to the *philosophia perennis* or *religio perennis*: one finds two types of people attracted to it. There are those who are already say, Catholics or Muslims, and who find that the insights of the *religio perennis* produce a deepening and an essentialization of their pre-existing faith; and there are those—possibly products of the post-religious modern world—who have discovered and been conquered by the *religio perennis*, and who as a result embrace, say, Catholicism or Islam in order sincerely to live, actualize, or realize, the truth or the truths that they have discovered. The first group are Catholics or Muslims first and *religio perennis* second; the second group are *religio perennis* first and Catholics or Muslims second. Those in the first category already possessed something of value, something sacred;

as a result, they may hesitate to embrace fully all the theses of the *religio perennis*. Those in the second category, on the other hand, owe everything to the *religio perennis*; absolutely nothing else could have awakened them to the sacred and distanced them from the illusions of the modern world; as a result, they may hesitate to embrace fully all the secondary demands of the denomination they have adopted, especially those of a communal or partisan nature.

These two positions are to some extent extremes; there are many positions that lie between them. Also, the two positions are not necessarily unchanging. Sometimes a person, who has come to Christianity through the *religio perennis*, slips into the life of his denomination, and "metaphysics", "universalism", etc., cease to be in the forefront of his spiritual life. Sometimes, on the other hand, a person who has been a "denominationalist", suddenly or gradually sees the full meaning of the *religio perennis*, is overwhelmed by its luminosity, crystallinity, and celestiality, and henceforth his sacramental and prayer life is governed, so to speak, by it alone. When all is said and done, however, one has to say that the two approaches do remain distinct, and each has its own characteristics and consequences.

Let me say here a word of criticism regarding the Vatican II Council of 1960-1965. It is not necessary to be a perennialist in order to condemn the official Roman Church of today; it is sufficient simply to know the traditional Catholic catechism. The discrepancy between the two is striking. The perennialist sympathizes with the most exoteric of Roman Catholics, provided he be orthodox. But he himself is not a Roman Catholic exoterist. The Catholic exoterist dreams of the "Catholicism of the nineteen-thirties", he gives his allegiance to a denomination, to a form. In so doing, he has much justification, for Catholicism in its historic, outward form endured to beyond the middle of the 20th century. There have been many important and remarkable saints in recent times: in the 19th century, St. Thérèse of Lisieux, St. Jean-Baptiste Vianney (the Curé d'Ars), St Bernadette of Lourdes and, in the 20th century, St. Maria Goretti.

Nevertheless, in spite of this unbroken tradition of dogma, sacrament, and sanctity, it is important to be aware that the Catholic Church of the nineteen-thirties had long since incorporated within itself many fatal flaws, all deriving ultimately from its suicidal espousal of the vainglory of the Renaissance. The irruption of Protestantism is usually seen as a reaction against the sale of indulgences and other abuses, but it could also be said that Luther, who loved St. Paul and St. Augustine, was in his fashion a man of the Middle Ages who rebelled against the illogicality and treason of the Renaissance. The Reformation did not kill Catholicism; in fact it provoked the Council of Trent at which the Catholic Church went as far as it could towards putting its house in order, thus enabling it to maintain its witness for several more centuries. The death blow to the official Catholic Church was delivered only in the 20th century by Teilhard de Chardin and "Vatican II".

Such strong criticism of the present-day Catholic Church may come as a surprise to readers; but the situation was unquestionably foreseen by the last traditional Pope, Pius XII, when he said that the day was coming soon when the faithful would only be able to celebrate the holy sacrifice of the mass on the secret altar of the heart. Many thought that he was referring to the threat of outward persecution, but it could equally well be maintained that his words applied to the impending arrival of a falsified church and a falsified liturgy. Be that as it may, the perennialist or esoterist owes allegiance, not to a form as such, but only to the Holy Spirit, only to the supra-formal Truth. He knows the meaning of forms; he respectfully and humbly participates in sacred forms revealed to vehicle his salvation; but he knows that forms are but messengers of the Formless, and that the Formless or Supra-formal, of necessity, possesses on earth more than one system of forms. The extrinsic reason for this plurality is the great ethnic and psychological divisions of mankind. The intrinsic reason is that the Supra-formal is inexhaustible, and each successive revelation, in its outward form, manifests a fresh aspect thereof. In its outward form, I say, because each revelation, in its inward essence, does give access to, and does confer the grace of, the Formless. That is why each one saves. This reality is what Schuon has called the supra-formal, or transcendent, unity of the religions.

It has been emphasized that universalism does not imply the rejection of forms. Does it imply syncretism? The answer is "No". The doctrine of the transcendent or esoteric unity of the religions is not a syncretism, but a synthesis. What does this mean? It means that we must *believe* in all orthodox, traditional religions, but we can *practice* only one. Consider the metaphor of climbing a mountain. Climbers can start from different positions at the foot of the mountain. From these positions, they must follow the particular path that will lead them to the top. We can and must believe in the efficacy of all the paths, but our legs are not long enough to enable us to put our feet on two paths at once! Nevertheless, the other paths can be of some help to us. For example, if we notice that someone on a neighboring path has a particularly skillful way of circumventing a boulder, it may be that we can use the same skill to negotiate such boulders as may lie ahead of us on our own path. The paths as such, however, meet only at the summit. The religions are one only in God.

Perhaps I could say in passing that, while it is a grave matter to change one's religion, the mountain-climbing metaphor nevertheless illustrates what takes place when one does. One moves horizontally across the mountain and joins an alternative path, and at that point one starts climbing again. One does not have to go back to the foot of the mountain and start again from there.

*

* *

In this chapter, I have moved back and forward between the *religio perennis* and the current world-wide epidemic of ethnic and religious strife known as communalism. I have done so because both are significant phenomena of our time. The one is only too outward; the other is inward and in a sense hidden. As regards the apparently intractable communal rivalries, there is little outwardly that we as individuals can do. Inwardly, however, we can help in two ways, firstly by our prayers, and secondly—and as a function of our prayer—by deepening our understanding of the relationship between forms and the Formless, and of the relationship which, ideally, should exist between the several forms themselves. Each revealed belief system (with its corresponding way of worship) is a particular manifestation of the *religio perennis*. It is therefore no mistake to regard any one revelation as *the* revelation, as long as one is not "nationalistic" or "competitive" about it. In practice, however, it can be a difficult matter. How can one, at one moment, enjoin people to be committed "traditional" Christians, and then, the next moment, speak with equal respect of the religions of Krishna, Buddha, or Mohammed? Difficult indeed. But, in some way, it has to be done.

The basic cultural distinction made by the post-Christian world is still between Christendom and all the rest, but this is simply not a good enough analysis for the present age. The distinction that we have to make today is between believers and non-believers, between the "good" and the "bad"—irrespective of their revealed form. In so doing we need not be afraid of being called "judgemental"! Our daily experience shows us that there is none so judgemental as the secular humanist. He judges everything. The trouble is: he judges wrongly—with devastating effects for the community and the nation.

"Judge not that ye be not judged." This is a text that is too easily misinterpreted. It applies to our egoism, our subjectivism, our self-interest; it does not preclude the divine gift of objectivity, still less does it abolish truth. There is manifestly plenty for us to "judge"—and oppose: atheism, agnosticism, and everything that flows from the "Enlightenment" and the French Revolution. We passively tolerate so much that comes from satan ("rock" music, fashionable "-isms", sacrilegious entertainments, blasphemous art) and yet we think our culture is threatened if someone wears a form of dress or speaks a language different from our own. We must be sufficiently alert to discriminate between what comes from God (no matter how exotic its outward form) and what does not (no matter how familiar).

Our judgements must be totally divorced from denomination. We must be able to oppose the "bad" (even though they be of our own religion), and acclaim the "good" (even though they belong to a strange religion). This injunction may sound platitudinous, but almost no one follows it instinctively. We must be capable of the cardinally important intuition that *every religion*—be it Christianity, Hinduism, Buddhism, or Islam—*comes from God and every religion leads back to God*; in these latter days, we underestimate the "other religions" at our peril. Alas, very few (be they Christians, Muslims, Hindus, Buddhists, or anything else) are able to make this angelic leap of faith—for many bad reasons, as well as for one good reason, namely that each religion has within it a verse corresponding to "No man cometh to the Father but by Me". Each religion is an expression of the Absolute—the Logos—otherwise it would not be a religion, but a man-made ideology, with no power to save.

It is precisely this "absolute" in each religion that makes it a religion, but it is difficult for most people to realize the *simple* truth that the Absolute, being by definition supra-formal, must needs—within the formal world—espouse many forms. It cannot be otherwise, despite the providentially "absolutist" text within each religion. To understand this truth, at least theoretically, is the *first* necessity in the present age. But unfortunately, like so many good things, this area has been partially taken over by the devil, in the shape of the cults, the "new age" movement, etc. One might say that it is in this area above all that the teachings and elucidations of the perennialists have an indispensable role to play.

6. SIX FUNDAMENTAL FLAWS IN THE EVOLUTIONIST HYPOTHESIS

(1) Logical

The greater cannot come from the lesser.

(A biological example: The acorn gives rise to the oak-tree precisely because it already "is" an oak-tree. The acorn is not some nondescript "unicellular organ" or an ameba.)

(2) Physical (entropy; the second law of thermodynamics)

Complexity tends towards degradation. Systems naturally move to a greater degree of randomness. Things run down, not up; they proceed from a state of order to a state of disorder. Order does not emerge from disorder (or organization from disorganization). Order is conferred on disorder by the input of "information" ("intelligence"), and cannot arise by chance. "Intelligence" is not the *product* of disorder! Nothing has ever been known to contravene this law, but the evolutionary hypothesis contradicts it.

(3) Biological (the stability of species)

There is no conclusive evidence that one species ever changed into another. (If there were, evolutionists would trumpet it from the house-tops!) "Parents" have never been known to give rise to other than their own kind. (There is evidence only for *intra*-specific variation, not for the formation of *new*—and self-reproducing—species.) This is because of the fundamental "stability" of species. A species is a Platonic archetype. Evolutionists try to "blur" this as much as possible; some even deny the reality of species.

(4) Statistical (not enough time)

Evolution requires that there should have been a spontaneous generation of life, but the simplest of living cells is so complex that the probabilities of its coming into existence by chance cannot be expressed in meaningful figures.

No matter how much one extends—on a realistic basis—the time-scale envisaged, it is statistically impossible for the generation of life, and for evolution, to have taken place by chance in the time available.

(The rather fantastical theory that life "may have come from outer space" merely sets the problem one stage further back; it does not solve it.)

(5) Teleological (the argument from design)

"It is impossible that blind, deaf, and dumb evolution could have given rise to eye, ear, and voice."

"The miracle of consciousness did not arise from a heap of pebbles."

(6) Philosophical (the relativist pitfall)

The evolutionist hypothesis is fatally impaired by the well-known contradiction of *relativism*, often demonstrated by means of the statement "All men are liars." (If they are, then this statement, also made by a man, is false.) Specifically, in the present case: man, who is said to be evolving (and is therefore relative), cannot all of a sudden step out of the evolutionary process, take up a stationary position, and dare to make *absolute* statements regarding the continuing process. It is this that is absurd.

For the theory of biological evolution to be sustainable, each one of the above objections must be refuted. This cannot be done. The evolutionists do not rise to this challenge. They look the other way, and bury their heads in the sand.

7. THE FLAWS OF DEMOCRACY

How can one possibly think that the counting of a million empty heads can be a way of reaching wisdom, or a sound and reasonable method for choosing a government? George Washington was one amongst many who clearly saw the fallacy of this, and yet it seems to be the very basis and definition of democracy.

Lest it be thought that my rhetorical question smacks of arrogance, let me say right away that these "heads" are by no means empty in all respects: on the contrary, some of them are carpenters, some are shoemakers, some are architects, some are doctors. Each one of them, far from being an "empty-head", is an expert, a specialist, a "master"—but only in his respective field. The point is that they are not "masters" of statecraft—or of religion. Yet it is precisely in these two domains, each of supreme importance, that every one of us is most ready to deliver his—very frequently untutored and unqualified—opinions. If I were prevailed upon to make a table, it would, alas, be a very strange table; and let no one ask me to make a pair of boots.

Continuing with the shoemaker metaphor, it is commonly said (in support of democracy) that "only the wearer knows where the shoe pinches", and therefore wearers have the right to speak. Well, yes, but this wise saying does not imply that the wearer can make his own shoes. It implies that he go to a master shoemaker who can make him a pair of shoes that fits; it implies that it is reasonable and normal for us to turn to one whom we know to have served his apprenticeship, achieved his mastership, or become an adept in the appropriate field. Can this be said of those who, hastily and unwisely, offer us opinions on politics or religion?

In olden times, the question did not arise: the Church (with an "infallible" pope) and the king (with a "divine right") told us what to believe, and what to do. It is hardly necessary to say that the meaning and nature of spiritual infallibility and temporal legitimacy are totally incomprehensible and totally abhorrent to modern man. Nevertheless, these mysteries have been thoroughly expounded and explained by philosophers from Plato to Thomas Aquinas, and it is not my intention to delve into them here. What one must understand, however, is that the existence, in modern times, of free choice in religion and free elections in regard to government is quite extraordinary and entirely novel.

This new freedom is universally seen as a boon, whereas in reality it is an intolerable imposition. How can one possibly give an opinion on religion if one is unable to figure out for oneself what is God and what is man? Does one know better than Revelation (something which is now ignored, or at best marginalized)? How can one give an opinion on government, when one does not know the nature and inherent laws either of the individual or of the collectivity? One should no more be asked to do this than one should be asked (if one is not a shoemaker) to make a pair of shoes.

The most visible flaw of democracy is in fact fairly well known: it is that the electorate will unfailingly vote for the candidate who promises them the greatest pecuniary advantage. Let no one say that this applies only in the case of an "unsophisticated" electorate. A "sophisticated electorate" is a contradiction in terms.

Another flaw of democracy is also becoming more and more apparent, namely, that it does not necessarily lead to the liberal utopia that its advocates have in mind. According to Thomas Jefferson, the third president of the United States, democracy is a system in which 51% of the people have the power to take away the privileges of the other 49%. For example, in a large number of places, democracy has led to the domination of one ethnic or religious community over another: Northern Ireland and contemporary Iraq are but two examples amongst many. Furthermore, the nazis in Germany, and the communists in post-war Czechoslovakia were voted into power under the democratic system. And one wonders what sort of régime would result, if democracy were applied in certain third-world countries. (Alas, one need not wonder. There have already been all too many examples.) In no way can democracy be relied on to produce equity or justice.

Another significant fact—often overlooked—is that there never has been a case, nor can there be a case, of *literal* democracy. Real power is always in the hands of a small élite or coterie, which most often is hidden from public view. It is small wonder that democracy has frequently been called "an elected dictatorship".

Neither corruption nor hypocrisy is new to mankind, but democracy has had more than its fair share of both. Experience in many countries has shown that there are few selfless politicians, and when anything bad is proposed, or carried out, it is invariably done in the name of democracy.

Some of the observations made above remain within the realm of what might be called the "Platonic ideal", while others are down-to-earth, and exceedingly pessimistic. We are now in the 21st century, and one may reasonably ask what, in the face of such pessimism, can possibly be the practical consequences of these considerations for us today? Is there any remedy, is there any alternative?

Alas, the answer too must be pessimistic. Even the best conservative philosophers of today cannot and do not offer a remedy, or propose an alternative system. For one thing, even if it were desirable, the past cannot be re-created. What is paramount is that we look implacably, objectively, and fearlessly at our modern world, and seek at least to *understand*. Understanding is strength—and more so than one may think. Burying one's head in the sand avails us naught. Understanding can even lead to an unexpected "solution", even if this be only inward.

In his article "What is Conservatism?" Titus Burckhardt concludes: "Since nearly all traditional forms in life are now destroyed, it is seldom possible for man to engage in a wholly useful and meaningful activity. But every loss spells gain: the disappearance of forms serves as a trial, and calls for a discernment; and the confusion in the surrounding world is a summons to turn, by-passing all accidents, to the essential." At a very profound level, this is a message of hope.

Democracy passes into despotism
—Plato (427-347 B.C).

Let not the cobbler judge above his last.
—Pliny (23-79)

Of all forms of government, democracy is the least accounted amongst civilized nations.
—George Washington (1732-1799)

A democracy is never more that mob rule, where 51% of the people may take away the privileges of the other 49%.
—Thomas Jefferson (1743-1826)

The best argument against democracy is a five-minute conversation with the average voter.
—Winston Churchill (1874-1965)

II.

Remembering (*theory*)

"Ye shall know the Truth"

John, 8, 32

8. WHAT IS RELIGION?

In terms of etymology, religion is that which binds, specifically, that which binds man to God. Religion engages man in two ways: firstly, by explaining the nature and meaning of the universe, or "justifying the ways of God to man" (this is theodicy); and secondly, by elucidating man's role and purpose in the universe, or teaching him how to liberate himself from its limitations, constrictions, and terrors (this is soteriology).

In the first place, religion is a doctrine of unity: God is one, and it is He who is the origin and final end of the universe and of man in it. Man, however, has become separated from God—through the "Fall" according to Christianity, through "ignorance" according to the Aryan religions. Consequently, religion is also a way of "return", a method of union. It is a sacramental path, a means of salvation.

Whatever they may be called, these two components are always present: theodicy and soteriology; doctrine and method; theory and practice; dogma and sacrament; unity and union.

Doctrine, or theory, concerns the mind (or, at the highest level, the "intellect", in the precise metaphysical sense of the Medieval *Intellectus*, the Greek *Nous*, or the Sanskrit *Buddhi*); method, or practice, concerns the will. Religion, to be itself, must always engage both mind and will.

The second, or practical, component of religion may be broken into two: namely, worship and morality. Worship, the sacramental element properly so-called, generally takes the form of participation in the revealed rites (public or private) of a given religion, with a view to conforming man's will to the norms of the Absolute, in other words, to the will of God. Morality, the social element, is "doing the things which ought to be done, and not doing the things which ought not to be done". Some of the contents of morality are universal: "thou shalt not kill", "thou shalt not steal", etc.; and some of the contents are specific to the religion in question: "thou shalt not make a graven image", "whom God hath joined together, let no man put asunder", etc.

We have thus reached the three elements which René Guénon considered to be the defining features of every religion: dogma, worship, and morality. When raised to a higher or more intense degree, namely that of spirituality or mysticism, they become, in the words of Frithjof Schuon: truth, spiritual way, and virtue. The purpose of a spiritual way is the assimilation or realization of divine truth—in other words effectively to know and love God.

*

*   *

The most important single point about religion is that it is not man-made. Religion is not invented by man, but revealed by God. Each religion is a unique revelation of Ultimate Reality. Divine revelation is a *sine quâ non*; without it, there is no religion, only man-made ideology, in which there is no guarantee of truth and above all no sacramental or salvational means.

The next important fundamental is tradition. Having once been revealed, religion is then handed down—unchanged in essence, but often increasingly elaborated in expression—from one generation to the next, by the power of tradition. And finally, closely linked with tradition, comes the attribute of orthodoxy, which is viewed as the principle of truth, or, at the practical level, the preservation of doctrinal purity.

In summary: religion's essential contents comprise dogma, worship, and morality; and religion's indispensable "container" or framework comprises revelation, tradition, and orthodoxy.

9. WHAT IS ORTHODOXY?

Nowadays, more often than not, orthodoxy is considered to be simply a form of intolerance: one set of people imposing their own views on others. In this connection, however, it is useful to recall the first item on the "Eightfold Path" of Buddhism: this is "right views" or "right thinking". It is obvious why "right thinking" should enjoy pride of place, for, both logically and practically, it is prior to "right doing". And what is the English word (derived from Greek) that signifies "right thinking"? None other than "orthodoxy".

To take the matter further: 2 + 2 = 4 is orthodox; 2 + 2 = 5 is unorthodox. Rather simple—but it also works the same way at much loftier levels. Another way of looking at it is this: even in the circumstances of today, many people still preserve the notion of "moral purity", and lay high value on it. Orthodoxy is "intellectual purity", and as such is an indispensable prelude to grace. Seen in this way—and far from "telling others what to believe"—orthodoxy is no more than a reference to the primacy and priority of truth. Orthodoxy, indeed, is the principle of truth that runs through the myths, symbols, and dogmas which are the very language of revelation.

Like morality, orthodoxy may be either universal (conformity to truth as such) or specific (conformity to the forms of a given religion). It is universal when it declares that God is uncreated, or that God is absolute and infinite. It is specific when it declares that Jesus is God (Christianity), or that God takes the triple form of Brahmâ, Vishnu, and Shiva (Hinduism).

Departure from orthodoxy is heresy: either intrinsic (for example, atheism or deism), or extrinsic (for example, an adherent of a Semitic religion rejecting the divinities of the Hindu and Greek pantheons).

Orthodoxy is normal, heresy abnormal. This permits the use of a medical metaphor: the study of the various traditional orthodoxies is the affair of the religious physiologist, whereas the study of heresies (were it worthwhile) is the affair of the religious pathologist.

The notion of orthodoxy is particularly important in a world in which the great religions have become explicitly aware of one another, and in which their adherents often live cheek by jowl. It is similarly important in the field of comparative religion. This point has been well expressed by Bernard Kelly:

Confusion is inevitable whenever cultures based on profoundly different spiritual traditions intermingle without rigid safeguards to preserve their purity. The crusader with the cross emblazoned on his breast, the loincloth and spindle of Mahatma Gandhi when he visited Europe, are images of the kind of precaution that is reasonable when traveling in a spiritually alien territory. The modern traveler in his bowler hat and pin stripes is safeguarded by that costume against any lack of seriousness in discussing finance. Of more important safeguards he knows nothing. The complete secularism of the modern Western world, wherever its influence has spread, has opened the floodgates to a confusion which sweeps away the contours of the spirit. . . . Traditional norms . . . provide the criteria of culture and civilization. Traditional orthodoxy is thus the pre-requisite of any discourse at all between the Traditions themselves.[1]

[1] *Dominican Studies* (London), vol. 7, 1954, p. 256.

10. WHAT IS THE INTELLECT?

In modern, everyday parlance, the word "intellect" is carelessly used as a synonym for "mind". Traditionalist authors, on the contrary, following a Medieval Scholastic usage, employ the word in a different and special sense; sometimes the initial letter of the word is capitalized. "Intellect" is said to be synonymous with "Spirit". What, then, is "Intellect" or "Spirit"?

The Intellect is the faculty of innate, objective knowledge. Examples of this knowledge, immediately apparent, and built into the human substance, are: our sense of logic, our capacity for arithmetic, our sense of justice, and our sense of right and wrong. Even a child knows how to reason, how to do arithmetic, knows what is fair or unfair, and knows what is right or wrong. These faculties, together with what is called our "conscience", all pertain to the Intellect.

The characteristics of the Intellect are immediacy, objectivity, and supra-formality or supra-individuality. The operation of the Intellect is sometimes called "intellectual intuition" or "intellection".

Everyone knows that man comprises soul and body; but in fact man is a ternary: he comprises Spirit (= Intellect), soul, and body. In the Middle Ages, this ternary was called *Spiritus, anima, corpus.* The soul is immortal, but at the same time it is formal, individual, and subjective. The Spirit or Intellect is immortal, and it is also supra-formal, universal, and objective.

Symbolically speaking, the seat of the intellect is, not the brain, but the heart. This is also appreciated at the popular level, as is shown by the spontaneous existence of such sayings as "I knew in my heart that . . . " or "I knew it in my heart". Intellectual knowledge is indeed sometimes called "Heart-Knowledge".

Further clear indications, at the popular level, of the distinction between Intellect and soul are to be found in such sayings as "I was ashamed of myself" and "I could have kicked myself". In the former saying, who is ashamed, and who is the "myself" of whom this person is ashamed? In the latter saying, who is doing the kicking, and who is being kicked? In each case, the first element is the Intellect, and the second element is the soul. In these examples, the Intellect is closely linked with the voice of conscience.

Above all, the Intellect is the faculty which enables man to conceive the Absolute, and to know the Truth. It is the source of his capacity for objectivity, of his ability—in contradistinction from the animals—to free himself from imprisonment in subjectivity. It is the very definition of the human state. As Frithjof Schuon has said more than once: "The Intellect can know all that is knowable." This is because Heart-Knowledge or *gnôsis* is innate, and fully present within us in a state of virtuality. This virtuality has to be realized, and this process corresponds to the Platonic doctrine of "recollection" (*anamnesis*), which in the last analysis is one with the Christian practice of the "remembrance of God" (*memoria Dei*). "The Kingdom of Heaven is within you."

Intellect and Spirit are the two sides of the same coin, the former pertaining to the theoretical or the doctrinal, and the latter pertaining to the practical or realizational. They pertain respectively to the objective (or discriminative) and the subjective (or unitive) modes of knowing.

The three elements or "levels" in the human constitution may be summarized as follows:

English	Latin	Greek	Arabic
Spirit (Intellect)	*Spiritus* (*Intellectus*)	*Pneuma* (*Nous*)	*Rûh* (*'Aql*)
soul	*anima*	*psyche*	*nafs*
body	*corpus*	*soma*	*jism*

It was indicated how modern usage confuses "intellectual" with "mental" or "rational". In fact, unlike the Intellect, which is "above" the soul, the mind or the reason is a content of the soul, as are the other human faculties such as will, affect or sentiment, imagination, and memory. Thus:

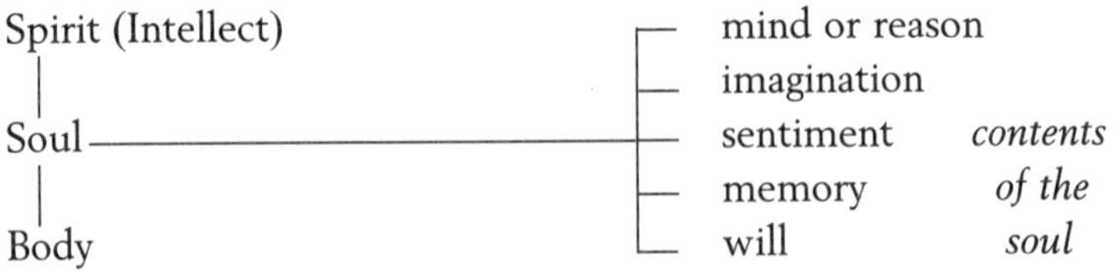

The Spirit, although "created", is supra-formal or universal, and is directly touched by the Divine. It is the only supra-individual, "archetypal", or objective element in man's constitution. The Spirit is therefore the "measure" of the soul; the soul can never be the "measure" of the Spirit. The fundamental error of psychologists such as Jung is their failure to distinguish between soul and Spirit, and consequently their "abolition" of Spirit. At one stroke this abolishes the capacity for objectivity and, by the same token, for spirituality. The chaos and damage resulting from this fatal and anti-Platonic act of blindness are incalculable.[1]

Let it be said right away that there is no impenetrable barrier between Intellect and mind: the relationship of the former to the latter is like the relationship of the pinnacle of a cone to its circumferential base. Metaphorically speaking, the majority of philosophers, since the end of the Middle Ages, have concerned themselves solely with the circumferential base, with little or no transcendent input in their thought. Henceforth the transcendent (previously known to be accessible either through revelation or intellection) has been regarded as mere "dogma" or "superstition". The result has been the tumultuous *dégringolade*, from Descartes—through Kant—to the present day, known as the "history of philosophy"! One miraculous exception to this cascading downwards was the Cambridge Platonists of the 17th century. The words of Virgil were never more applicable: *Facilis descensus Averni; sed revocare gradum, hic labor est!* ("The descent into Avernus is easy; but to recall one's steps, this is hard"!)

It is appropriate here to introduce some consideration of the Divinity. "Ordinary" theology speaks of God and man. On the other hand, mystical theology, or universal metaphysics—as evidenced, for example, by Shankara in Hinduism, Meister Eckhart in Christianity, and Ibn 'Arabî in Islam—makes a distinction, within God Himself, between "God" and "Godhead", between "Creator" and "Divine Essence", between "Personal God" and "Impersonal God", between "Being" and "Beyond-Being".

The Divinity is absolute, creation is relative. Nevertheless, within the Absolute (the Divine Essence), there is already a prefiguration of the relative, and this is the Personal God or Creator. This prefiguration of creation in the Uncreated is the "Uncreated Logos".

Furthermore, within creation, which is relative, there is a reflection of the Absolute, and this is the Spirit or Intellect. Objectively, this reflection of the Absolute within the relative (or of the Uncreated within the created) shows itself in such things as Truth, Beauty, Virtue, Symbol, and Sacrament. It also manifests in Prophet,

[1] Jung, unlike Freud, is often considered to be friendly to religion! This is a classic example of "a wolf in sheep's clothing"!

Redeemer, *Tathâgatha*, *Avatâra*. This reflection of the Absolute in the relative is the "created Logos".[2]

Without the Logos (with its two "Faces", created and uncreated), no contact between man and God would be possible. This seems to be the position of the Deists. Without the Logos, there would be a fundamental dualism, and not "Non-dualism" (*Advaita*) as the Vedantists call it. The doctrine and the role of the Logos can be expressed in diagrammatic form as follows:

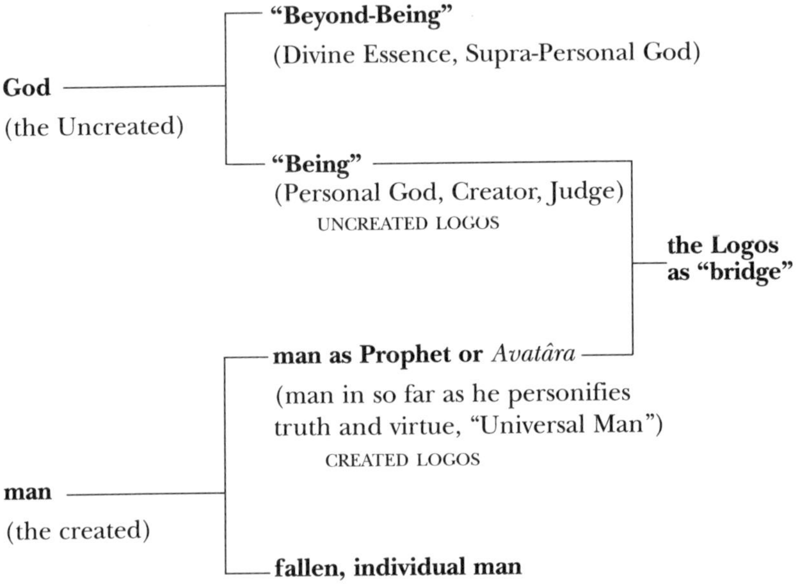

The spiritualities or mysticisms of all of the great religions teach that it is by uniting himself (in prayer and sacrament) with the "created Logos", that man attains to union with God.

In perceiving, within man, the three levels *Spiritus*, *anima*, and *corpus*, and in perceiving, within God, the two levels Personal Creator and Divine Essence, we have reached five levels. These have been called the "Five Levels of Reality" or the "Five Divine Presences". These levels, their meaning, and their relationships, are laid forth in the following table:

[2] This exposition is taken from the writings of Frithjof Schuon. See in particular *Esoterism as Principle and as Way* (Perennial Books, London, 1981).

The Five Levels of Reality

<table>
<tr><td colspan="3" rowspan="2">The Divine

The Unmanifest
The Uncreated
The Metacosmic</td><td colspan="2">(1) BEYOND-BEING

(the Divine Essence, the Supra-Personal God)</td><td>ABSOLUTE</td><td>ÂTMÂ</td><td rowspan="2">DIVINE</td><td rowspan="3">HEAVEN</td><td rowspan="4">IMMORTAL</td></tr>
<tr><td>(2) BEING

(the Personal God, Creator, Judge; Divine Qualities)</td><td>UNCREATED LOGOS</td><td rowspan="4">RELATIVE</td><td rowspan="4">MÂYÂ</td></tr>
<tr><td rowspan="3">EXISTENCE

The Manifest
The Created
The Cosmic</td><td colspan="2">Universal or Supra-formal Manifestation</td><td>(3) Spirit, Intellect

(Spiritual, Intellectual, or Angelic realm)</td><td>CREATED LOGOS</td><td rowspan="3">HUMAN</td></tr>
<tr><td rowspan="2">individual or formal manifestation</td><td>subtle</td><td colspan="2">(4) soul

(animic or psychic realm)</td><td rowspan="2">EARTH</td></tr>
<tr><td>gross</td><td colspan="2">(5) body

(corporeal realm)</td><td>MORTAL</td></tr>
</table>

It may be useful to indicate the origin and precise meaning of the concepts "subjective" and "objective". The most direct key in this regard is the Hindu appellation for the Divinity: *Sat-Chit-Ânanda.* This expression is usually translated as "Being-Consciousness-Bliss". This is accurate, and permits one to see that "Being" is the Divine Object (God Transcendent or Ultimate Reality) and that "Consciousness" is the Divine Subject (God Immanent or the Supreme Self), while "Bliss"—the harmonious coming-together of the two—is Divine Union. The most fundamental translation therefore of *Sat-Chit-Ânanda* is "Object-Subject-Union". This is the model, or origin, of all possible objects and subjects, and of the longing of the latter for the former. With this in mind, it can be seen that *Sat-Chit-Ânanda* may also be translated as "Known-Knower-Knowledge" or "Beloved-Lover-Love".[3] (*See the table on p. 122.*)

The terms "objective" and "subjective" are in themselves "neutral". The term "subjective" only takes on a pejorative meaning when the subject in question is irrational.

[3] With a spiritual or "operative" intention in mind, it may also be translated as "Invoked-Invoker-Invocation".

11. FRITHJOF SCHUON AND THE PERENNIALIST SCHOOL

What has become known as the "perennialist" school of thought was founded by the French philosopher and orientalist René Guénon (1886-1951) and brought to full fruition by the German philosopher and poet Frithjof Schuon (1907-1998). It may be of interest to recall in passing that two other celebrated wisdom schools had dual originators, namely, those associated with Socrates and Plato in 5th-century B.C. Athens, and with Rûmî and Shams ad-Dîn Tabrîzî in 13th-century Turkey. The two leading continuators of this current of intellectuality and spirituality were the German-Swiss Titus Burckhardt (1908-1984) and Anglo-Indian Ananda Coomaraswamy (1877-1947).

Even though virtually all of Schuon's books have been available in English for many years, one cannot say that his name is a familiar one to the general public. To people with special interests, however, in such fields as comparative religion, metaphysics, theology, and the spiritual life, a great deal has been known about him for a long time.[1] Fifty years ago, an English Thomist wrote of Schuon: "His work has the intrinsic authority of a contemplative intelligence".[2] More recently, a senior American academic declared: "In depth and breadth, the paragon of our time. I know of no living thinker who begins to rival him."[3] T. S. Eliot's perception was similar. Regarding Schuon's first book, he wrote in 1953: "I have met with no more impressive work in the comparative study of Oriental and Occidental religion."

The term "perennial philosophy" has existed since the Renaissance, but in modern times it became familiar to the English-speaking world thanks to the book of the same name by Aldous Huxley.[4] The central idea of the perennial philosophy is that Divine Truth is one,

[1] For full biographical information on Schuon, see *Frithjof Schuon: Life and Teachings* by Jean-Baptiste Aymard and Patrick Laude (SUNY, Ithaca NY, 2004).

[2] Bernard Kelly, in *Dominican Studies* (London), vol. 7, 1954.

[3] Emeritus Professor Huston Smith, 1974.

[4] Huxley himself was not a perennialist or traditionalist. His anthology under this name is not without interest, but his own viewpoint is superficial and confused.

timeless, and universal, and that the different religions are but different languages expressing that one Truth. In the Renaissance, the term betokened the recognition of the fact that the philosophies of Pythagoras, Plato, Aristotle, and Plotinus incontrovertibly expounded the same truths as lay at the heart of Christianity. Subsequently the meaning of the term was enlarged to cover the metaphysics and mysticisms of all of the great world religions, notably, Hinduism, Buddhism, and Islam.

In other words, a fundamental concept of the perennialist school is that of "the transcendent unity of the religions"—the very title of Schuon's first book. It affirms that, at the center of each religion, there is a core of truth (about God and man, prayer and morality) which is identical. The various world religions are indeed different: this precisely is their reason for being. It is their essential core that is identical, not the outward form. All the great world religions were revealed by God, and it is because of this that each one speaks in such an absolute fashion. If it did not do so, it would not be a religion, nor would it offer any means of salvation. Later in this chapter, we will describe each of the main tenets of metaphysics and spirituality, as expounded in the writings of Frithjof Schuon.

Schuon wrote more than twenty books in French. All were in the realm of religion and spirituality—covering both East and West—but in tone they were highly philosophical, or sapiential. His predecessors in writing were not directly St. Augustine, St. Bernard of Clairvaux or St. Francis of Assisi, nor even Meister Eckhart; rather they were Shankara, Pythagoras, and Plato. That is not to say that Schuon's writings are non-mystical, or lacking in poetic and spiritual grace; but unquestionably they are philosophical in mode and style. They expound truths, and provide answers to age-old questions; but they also evoke spirituality, and indicate the way of salvation.

Schuon's remarkable books include *The Transcendent Unity of the Religions*, *Logic and Transcendence*, *Esoterism as Principle and as Way*, *Language of the Self* (on Hinduism), *Treasures of Buddhism*, and *Understanding Islam*. His beautiful last book, *The Transfiguration of Man* is like a synthesis of his life's work.

Schuon wrote only two books in his native German. One was his very first book, published in 1935 and entitled *Leitgedanken zur Urbesinnung*, which basically means "Themes to aid Primordial Meditation". The other was his memoirs: *Erinnerungen und Betrachtungen* ("Memories and Meditations"), which was conceived as a private document, and remains unpublished. During his childhood and youth, however, Schuon wrote poems in German. These early poems, though charming, and bearing witness to a profound and sensitive soul, were never published in full. After a space of many years—in fact during the last two and a half years of his ninety-year life—Schuon returned to his poetic vocation, and composed over three thousand didactic poems in twenty-three "collections". This amazing poetic cycle has been published in its entirety in the original German, and also in English and French translations.

Before going any further, let it be reiterated that, for Schuon, philosophy (a "love of wisdom") was represented by such as Pythagoras, Plato, Aristotle, and the Medieval Scholastics, and came to an abrupt end with Descartes, Kant, and their successors. For Schuon, philosophy was a wisdom born of certainty, not a skepticism born of doubt. It was not a "search" for answers to badly-put questions, but an exposition of eternal Truth—that "wisdom uncreate" (as St. Augustine called it) which is commonly known as the *philosophia perennis.* This is the *sancta sophia* which the Bible describes in these words: "From the beginning and before the world, was I created, and unto the world to come I shall not cease to be."

Let us now say some words on the "pioneer" of the perennialist school, the Frenchman René Guénon, whose books Schuon discovered in 1924, when he was seventeen. Schuon already had a profound metaphysical (that is to say, Platonic) vision of God and man, but Guénon's writings provided him with the vocabulary or terminology by means of which he could give precise expression to his insights. A few years later, Schuon wrote his first letter to Guénon, and, for the rest of Guénon's life, he maintained an intimate correspondence with him. He also visited Guénon in Cairo in 1938 and 1939. From the early 1930s onwards, Schuon gradually acquired a small group of like-minded friends—in Basle, Paris, and elsewhere—who were moved by the "Guénonian" and "Schuonian" viewpoint.

Guénon traced the origin of what he called the modern deviation to the ending of the Middle Ages and the arrival of the Renaissance, that cataclysmic inrush of secularization, when nominalism vanquished realism, individualism (or humanism) replaced universalism, and empiricism banished scholasticism. An important part of Guénon's work was therefore his critique of the modern world from an implacably "Platonic" or metaphysical point of view. This was fully expounded in his two masterly volumes *The Crisis of the Modern World* and *The Reign of Quantity and the Signs of the Times.* The affirmative side of Guénon's work was his exposition of the immutable principles of universal metaphysics and traditional orthodoxy. His main source was the Shankaran doctrine of "non-duality" (*advaita*), and his chief work in this respect is *Man and his becoming according to the Vedanta.* However, he also turned readily to other traditional sources, since he considered all traditional forms to be various expressions of the one supra-formal Truth. Another important aspect of Guénon's work was his brilliant exposition of the intellectual content of traditional symbols, from whichever religion they might come. See in this connection his *Fundamental Symbols of Sacred Science.*

It is important to note that Guénon's writings, decisively important though they were, were purely "theoretical" in character, and made no pretense of dealing with the question of spiritual realization. In other words, they were generally concerned with intellectuality (or doctrine) and not directly with spirituality (or method).

Schuon continued, in even more notable fashion, the perspicacious and irrefutable critique of the modern world of Guénon, and reached unsurpassable heights in his exposition of the essential truth—illuminating and saving—that lies at the heart of every revealed form. Schuon called this supra-formal truth the *religio perennis.* This term, which does not imply a rejection of the similar term *philosophia perennis,* nevertheless contains a hint of an additional dimension which is unfailingly present in Schuon's writings. This is that intellectual understanding entails a spiritual responsibility, that intelligence requires to be complemented by sincerity and faith, and that "seeing" (in height) implies "believing" (in depth). In other words, the greater our perception of essential and saving truth, the greater our obligation towards an effort of inward or spiritual "realization".

As with Guénon, Schuon's style of writing, although original and poetic, was extremely impersonal in tone. He wrote as a Vedantist or a Platonist, and not in the name of a particular religion. His viewpoint was, that whereas one must believe in all of the great religions—as several expressions of the one Truth—one should, and indeed one can, follow or practice, only one.

René Guénon (1886-1951)

Frithjof Schuon (1907-1998)

Ananda K. Coomaraswamy (1877-1947)

Titus Burckhardt (1908-1984)

We may note also that, from his youth onwards, Frithjof Schuon was an artist. In his early years, his artistic activity mostly took the form of beautiful sketches of the heads of men of a variety of ethnicities: Chinese, Hindu, Arab, and Red Indian. These portrayed above all the qualities of rigor and dignity. In his middle life, Schuon created many beautiful canvases with Red Indian themes. A little later he produced many paintings of the Virgin Mary. These were not in the style of traditional Christian paintings (Eastern Church icons, Catalan frescoes, Celtic, Mozarabic, or Ethiopian book illuminations), but rather reflected a "Hindu"-style inspiration, and consisted of images somewhat reminiscent of a Hindu Goddess. Reproductions of all styles of Schuon's art were published in a book entitled *Images of Primordial and Mystic Beauty.*

The works of Guénon and Schuon did not remain unnoticed. Almost immediately, they gave rise to the two great "continuators" mentioned above, namely, the Anglo-Indian Ananda K. Coomaraswamy, who wrote in English, and the German Swiss Titus Burckhardt, who wrote in both German and French. Let us therefore, before reviewing the key elements in Schuon's teachings, say a few words about each of them.

The illustrious scholar Ananda Coomaraswamy (1877-1947) was an authority on the art and esthetics of both East and West. His vast erudition enabled him to demonstrate in fascinating detail the manifold flowering of the traditional civilizations to which the great revelations gave rise. His principal early works were *Mediaeval Sinhalese Art* (1908), *The Dance of Shiva* (1912), *Myths of the Hindus and Buddhists* (1927), and *History of Indian and Indonesian Art* (1927). It was only relatively late in life that Coomaraswamy discovered the works of René Guénon but, despite his long-recognized celebrity as a scholar in his own right, he had the merit of allowing himself to be thoroughly penetrated by the Guénonian point of view. Thereafter several important traditionalist works flowed from Coomaraswamy's pen, including *Christian and Oriental or True Philosophy of Art* (1943), *Figures of Speech or Figures of Thought?* (1946), and *Am I My Brother's Keeper?* (1947). In these books Coomaraswamy masterfully expounded the Guénonian perspective.

Titus Burckhardt, a German-Swiss, was born in Florence in 1908 and died in Lausanne in 1984. In the age of modern science and technocracy, he was one of the most remarkable of the exponents of universal truth, in the realm of metaphysics as well as in the realm of cosmology and of traditional art. In a world of existentialism, psychoanalysis, and sociology, he was a major voice of the *philosophia perennis* that is expressed in Platonism, *Vedânta*, Sufism, Taoism, and other authentic esoteric or sapiential teachings.

Burckhardt's chief metaphysical exposition, beautifully complementing the work of Schuon, is *An Introduction to Sufi Doctrine*. This is an intellectual masterpiece which analyzes comprehensively and with precision the nature of esoterism as such. It begins by making clear, by a series of lucid and economical definitions, what esoterism is and what it is not, goes on to examine the doctrinal foundations of Islamic esoterism or Sufism, and ends with an inspired description of "spiritual alchemy" or the contemplative path that leads to spiritual realization.

Burckhardt had a particular affinity with traditional art and craftsmanship and was skilled in the evaluation of traditional architecture, iconography, and other arts and crafts. In particular, he dwelt on how they had been—and could be—turned to account spiritually, both as meaningful activities which by virtue of their inherent symbolism harbor a doctrinal message, and above all as supports for spiritual realization and means of grace. Burckhardt's main work in the field of art was his *Sacred Art in East and West*, which contains masterly chapters on the metaphysics and esthetics of Hinduism, Buddhism, Taoism, Christianity, and Islam, and ends with a useful and practical insight into the contemporary situation entitled "The Decadence and the Renewal of Christian Art". Other important works by Burckhardt were *Siena, City of the Virgin*, *Chartres and the Birth of the Cathedral*, and *Moorish Culture in Spain*.

*

* *

KEY ELEMENTS IN SCHUON'S METAPHYSICAL AND SPIRITUAL TEACHING

There are a number of key elements in Schuon's metaphysical and spiritual teaching with which one should be familiar in order fully to understand all his writings. These are reviewed one by one hereunder.

(1) The Distinction between the "Absolute" and the "Relative", between *Âtmâ* and *Mâyâ*, or between "Beyond-Being" and "Being"

(2) The Doctrine of the Logos

(3) The Three Spiritual Ways (or the Three Spiritual Temperaments)

(4) The Six Themes of Meditation

(5) The Five Levels of Reality (or the Five Divine Presences)

(6) The Four Ages

(7) The Four Social Stations (or the Four Castes)

(8) The Meaning of Race

*

* *

(1) The Distinction between the "Absolute" and the "Relative", between *Âtmâ* and *Mâyâ*, or between "Beyond-Being" and "Being"

The first of all "discriminations" or "discernments" in universal metaphysics, as expounded by Schuon, is that between *Âtmâ* and *Mâyâ*. It is essential to, and lies behind, all of his writings. Expressed in Vedantic terms, it is fundamentally the discernment between the Absolute (*Âtmâ*) and the Relative (*Mâyâ*). According to this doctrine—as represented variously by Shankara (Hinduism), Plato (Ancient Greece), Eckhart (Christianity), and Ibn 'Arabî (Islam)—only the Divine Essence ("Beyond-Being") is Absolute, whereas the Creator or Personal God ("Being"), as the first self-determination of the Divine Essence, is already within the domain of the relative. The Creator, nevertheless, is "absolute" with regard to His creation and, in view of this, is qualified by Schuon as the "*relatively absolute*". This term, although apparently illogical, harbors an important meaning.

(2) The Doctrine of the Logos

The Personal God ("Being"), as originator of creation, is "the prefiguration of the relative in the Absolute". Within creation, on the other hand, there is a "reflection of the Absolute in the relative", and this is the *Avatâra*, the Prophet, the Savior; it is also Truth; Beauty and Virtue; Symbol and Sacrament. This brings us to the doctrine of the Logos, with its two faces, created and uncreated. The "prefiguration of the relative in the Absolute" (the Creator or Personal God) is the uncreated Logos; the "reflection of the Absolute in the relative" (the *Avatâra*; Symbol, or Sacrament) is the created Logos. Thus the Logos, which with its two faces, created and uncreated, is the "bridge" between man and God, indicates clearly what is meant by a "means of salvation": the religious adherent, by uniting himself sacramentally with the created Logos, finds therein a means of uniting himself with the Uncreated: namely, God as such. This can perhaps be made clearer by means of the following diagram:

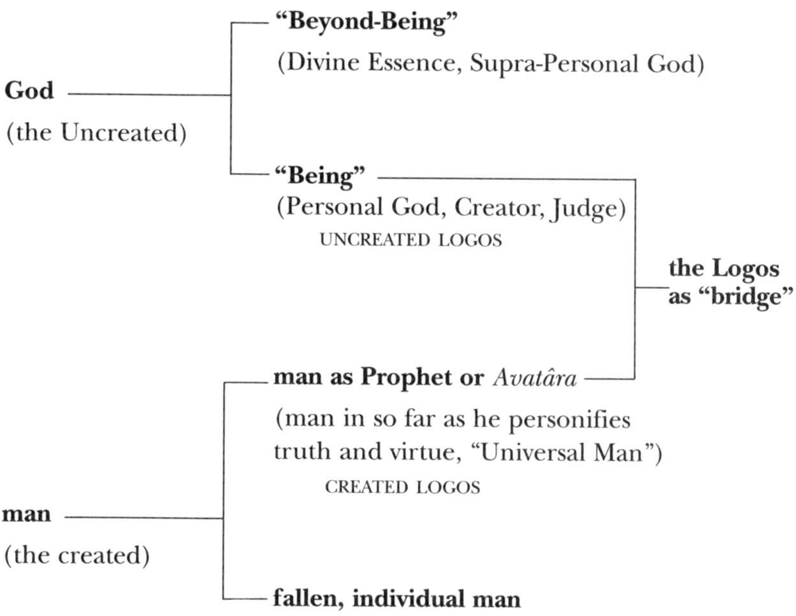

(3) The Three Spiritual Ways (or the Three Spiritual Temperaments)

Another important concept in Schuon's spiritual teaching are the three universal modes of the worship of God. In Hinduism, they are called *karma* (the Way of Action), *bhakti* (the Way of Devotion), and *jñâna* (the Way of Knowledge or Gnosis). In Islam, these are called *makhâfa* (Fear of God), *mahabba* (Love of God), and *ma'rifa* (Knowledge of God). Following an incident in the life of Christ, when he was lodged in the house of two sisters, the first of these ways (the Way of Action) is called in Christianity the "Way of Martha" whereas the Way of Contemplation (which comprises both the Way of Love and the Way of Knowledge) is called the "Way of Mary".

We take the opportunity to make clear that the Greek word *gnôsis* ("knowledge") is used here in an entirely orthodox and non-sectarian sense, and does not refer to the heretical "gnosticism" of the early centuries of Christianity. It is the same "gnosis" (*gnôsis Theou*, "Knowledge of God") as is found in the Gospels, in St. Paul (for example, in *Romans*, 11, 33), and in Clement of Alexandria. Schuon uses the noun gnostic to mean a "knower", in the sense of the Sanskrit term *jnânin*, namely one predisposed to follow the "Way of Knowledge".

It will have been noticed that Schuon has frequent recourse to concepts and terminology deriving from the non-Christian religions. It is hardly necessary to say that this in no way resembles the fantasies of "new age" thought. This practice is rendered possible by his intimate and encyclopedic knowledge of all the world religions, and is used by him in order accurately and succinctly to express certain spiritual and metaphysical concepts.

(4) The Six Themes of Meditation

Absolutely central to Schuon's spiritual teaching is what he calls the Six Themes of Meditation, which, throughout his writings, he has presented in a myriad of ways. Their very simplicity of structure is a sign of their high inspiration. They are based on the passive and active aspects of the three degrees of spirituality just referred to. Their most simple presentation is as follows:

The Six Themes of Meditation		
	passive mode	active mode
	1	2
Fear	renunciation, abstention	act, perseverance
	3	4
Love	resignation, gratitude	fervor, trust, generosity
	5	6
Knowledge	extinction, truth	union

Schuon has said that these six stations or virtues are both successive stages and simultaneous aspects, both a pre-condition and a result, of following a spiritual path or a way to salvation. He describes the Six Themes of Meditation in detail in the final chapter of *The Eye of the Heart* and in the final chapter of *Stations of Wisdom*.

(5) The Five Levels of Reality or the Five Divine Presences

Everyone knows the distinction between God and man, and within man, everyone knows the distinction between soul and body. We thus immediately have three "levels": God, soul, and body. Then there is the distinction (mentioned above) that exists within God Himself, namely, between the Divine Essence ("Beyond-Being") and God the Creator-Helper-Judge ("Being"). The Divine Essence and God the Creator constitute the first two of the five "levels"; they are Divine, and Uncreated. The soul and the body are the fourth and fifth levels; they are human, and created. The third or intermediate level is that of the Spirit or Intellect—it is the Logos in its created aspect. The terms creation and created are synonymous with the terms manifestation and manifested.

The human levels (the fourth and the fifth) constitute "formal manifestation", which comprises both subtle manifestation (soul) and gross manifestation (body). The third level, also created or manifested is "supra-formal or universal manifestation"; this is the spiritual or intellectual level (the latter term being understood in the Medieval or Scholastic sense).

The Divine levels (the first and the second) are Unmanifested or Uncreated.

The term "Intellect" must not be confused with "mind" (the faculty of discursive reason). The mind, along with the imagination, sentiment, and memory, is a content of the soul (*anima* or *psyche*).

The Spirit (Latin *Spiritus*, Greek *Pneuma*) or Intellect (Latin *Intellectus*, Greek *Nous*) corresponds to the "angelic" or "celestial" realm, the realm of the Platonic "Ideas". It represents the only "archetypal" or objective element in the constitution in man. (This use of the term "archetype" has nothing to do with the Jungian misuse of the term, where it designates sub-human elements of an obscure nature, and not, as in Platonism, supra-human elements, the nature of which is clarity). The "Intellect" is the "measure" of the soul; the soul can never be the "measure" of the Intellect. "Spirit" and "Intellect" are the two sides of the same coin, the latter pertaining to Truth (or doctrine), and the former to Reality (or spiritual realization). (*See the first table on p. 46.*)

The distinction between "Intellect" and "soul" is absolutely cardinal. The chaos of modern philosophy and modern psychology arises precisely from the confusion of these two and, as often as not, from the total loss of the concept of "Intellect". It is the abolition of the capacity for objectivity, which is the distinguishing feature of man, and the only thing that makes us truly human.

The doctrine of the Five Levels of Reality can be made clear with the help of the following diagram:

The Five Levels of Reality

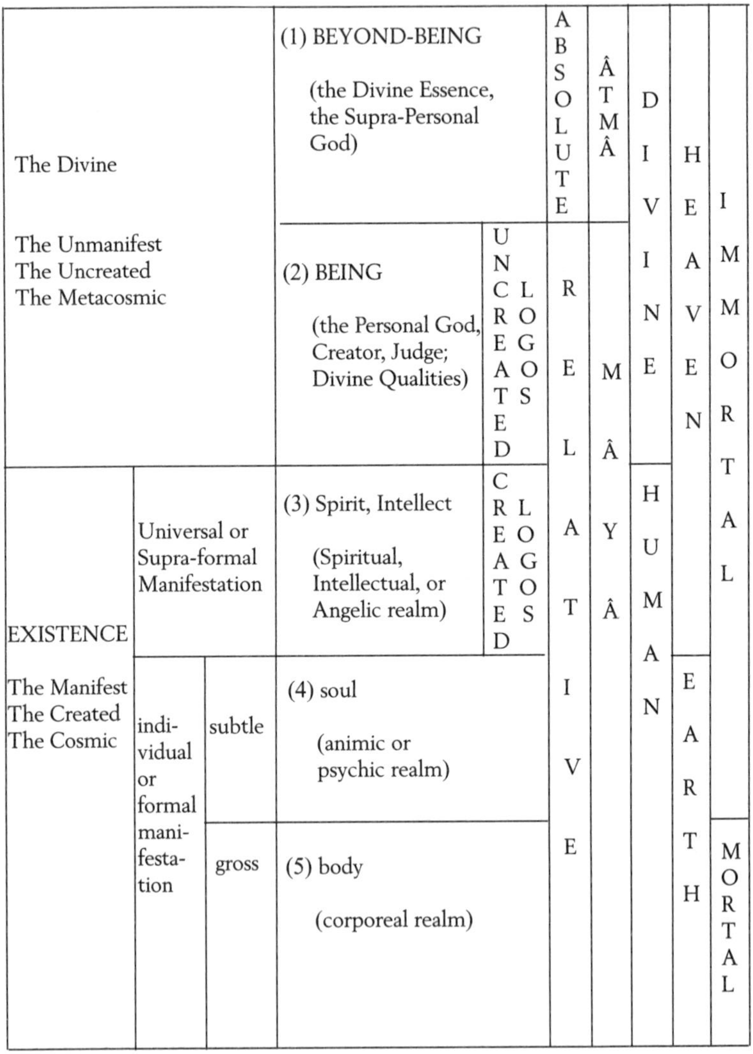

(6) The Four Ages

The four ages of humanity envisaged by classical antiquity were: the Golden Age, the Silver Age, the Bronze Age, and the Iron Age. The corresponding Hindu doctrine calls these the four *Yugas*. In terms of duration, these ages or *yugas* are said to be in the following proportion to one another:

Krita-Yuga (or *Satya-Yuga*)	Golden Age	4
Treta-Yuga	Silver Age	3
Dvapara-Yuga	Bronze Age	2
Kali-Yuga ("Dark Age")	Iron Age	1

The four ages represent a continual decline, extending from the creation to "the end of the world". The decline is not even, but—as suggested by the table above—gradually accelerates. This decline was pithily expressed by the late American Professor John Lodge, who is remembered for his saying (often quoted by Ananda Coomaraswamy): "From the stone age until now, *quelle dégringolade*! Similar doctrines are to be found in the Christian, Islamic, and Red Indian traditions. All of them speak of the "signs of the times", and describe them only too clearly. The Christian ones are well known, and the Islamic ones are similar. Both René Guénon and Frithjof Schuon take the view that humanity is now in the last phase of the *Kali-Yuga*, the "Dark Age".

A Hindu prophecy regarding the "last days", taken from the *Vishnu Purana* (3rd century A.D). is as follows:

> Riches and piety will diminish daily, until the world will be completely corrupted. In those days it will be wealth that confers distinction, passion will be the sole reason for union between the sexes, lies will be the only method for success in business, and women will be the objects merely of sensual gratification. The earth will be valued only for its mineral treasures, dishonesty will be the universal means of subsistence, a simple ablution will be regarded as sufficient purification. . . .
>
> The observance of castes, laws, and institutions will no longer be in force in the Dark Age, and the ceremonies prescribed by the *Vedas* will be neglected. Women will obey only their whims and will be infatuated with pleasure. . . . Men of all kinds will presumptuously regard themselves as the equals of *brahmins*. . . . The *vaishyas* will abandon agriculture and commerce and will earn their living by servitude or by the exercise of mechanical professions. . . . The path of the *Vedas* having been abandoned, and man having been led astray

> from orthodoxy, iniquity will prevail and the length of human life will diminish in consequence. . . . Then men will cease worshiping Vishnu, the Lord of sacrifice, Creator and Lord of all things, and they will say: "Of what authority are the *Vedas*? Who are the Gods and the *brahmins*? What use is purification with water?" The dominant caste will be that of *shûdras*. . . . Men, deprived of reason and subject to every infirmity of body and mind, will daily commit sins: everything which is impure, vicious, and calculated to afflict the human race will make its appearance in the Dark Age.

This is remarkably similar to the prophecy of St. Paul in *2 Timothy*, 3, 1-7:

> In the last days, perilous times shall come: men will love nothing but money and self; they will be arrogant, boastful, and abusive, with no respect for parents, no gratitude, no piety, no natural affection. . . . They will be men who put pleasure in the place of God, who preserve the outward form of religion, but are a standing denial of its reality. . . . Ever learning, but never able to come to a knowledge of the truth.

(7) The Four Social Stations (or the Four Castes)

Another doctrine which René Guénon and Frithjof Schuon accept is that of the four-fold "vertical" division of humanity, into four social "stations" or "castes". Historically speaking, this is rendered most explicit in the Hindu "caste system", but the reality of this differentiation is inherent in all society. The Hindu social system and the Medieval social system (the latter having left its traces in Western society to this day) can be indicated as follows:

sannyasins or *sadhus*	those who are *above* caste (monks, hermits)
(1) *brahmins*	"Lords Spiritual" (priests, those who are of spiritual or "intellectual" temperament) [sacerdotal caste]
(2) *kshatriyas*	"Lords Temporal" (kings, princes, those who are of noble temperament) [royal caste]
(3) *vaishyas*	"middle class" (farmers, craftsmen, merchants) ["third estate", bourgeoisie]
(4) *shudras*	"laboring class" (unskilled laborers, serfs) [proletariat]
chandalas or *pariahs*	those who are *below* caste (renegades, "drop-outs")

(8) The Meaning of Race

Schuon's view envisages that each of the great religions corresponds to the need of a particular human "receptacle", this being either a particular race or else a particular mentality which transcends one single race. This issue is too complex to elaborate here, but it is brilliantly laid forth, with amazing insight and detail, in his book *Castes and Races*. The following is a simplified table covering the principal races, languages, and religions:

A. Primary Races

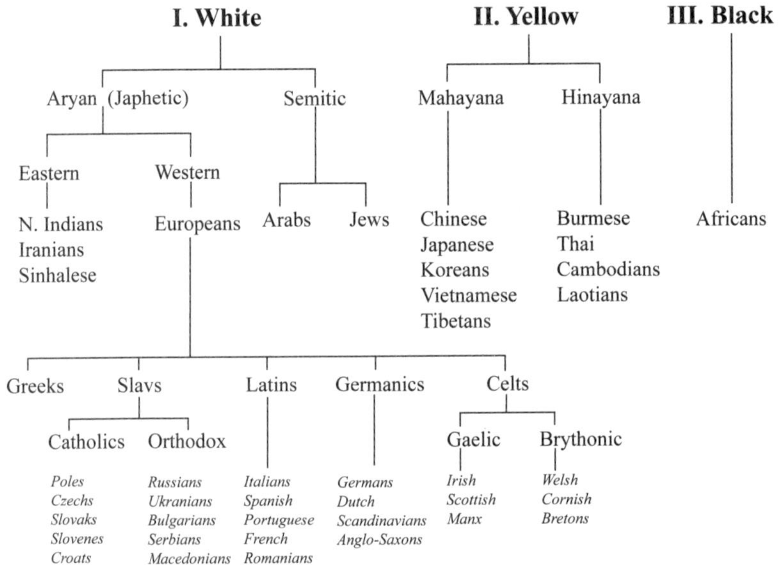

B. Intermediate Races

IV. Dravidians (S. Indians) (Equatorial branch of the White race)	V. Malay (Equatorial branch of the Yellow race)	VI. Red Indian (Intermediate race between Yellow and White)	VII. Black Hamites (Intermediate race between Black and White)
Tamil (Madras)	Malays	Native Americans	Somalis
Telegu (Andhra)	Indonesians		Ethiopians
Kannarese (Mysore)	Filipinos		
Malayalam (Kerala)			

12. THE MASCULINE AND THE FEMININE

Part I

(1) The masculine and the feminine have their origin in God Himself, the former being prefigured by God as the Absolute (or the Exclusive), and the latter being prefigured by God as the Infinite (or the Inclusive).
(2) It is only in the extreme differentiation of the masculine and the feminine that their respective natures are fully manifest. (This is irrespective of whether the relationship between them be regarded as hierarchical or complementary). The bliss (*ânanda*) that comes from the union of the masculine and the feminine depends precisely on their extreme differentiation. The bliss of union is diminished to the degree that this differentiation is impaired.
(3) Within the feminine, it is necessary to distinguish between the qualities pertaining to "Eve" (*Eva*), the temptress, and those pertaining to "Mary" (*Ave*), the Co-Redemptrix.
(4) Analogously, and taking our cue from the Islamic perspective, it is necessary, within "Eve", to distinguish between the "fallen" Eve and the "repentant" Eve.

It is perverse to ignore or oppose point (2) and pernicious not to take into account points (3) and (4). Both errors are characteristic of the modern age, and are part and parcel of "feminism".

*
* *

Several of the doctrines of Hinduism are relevant to the question of the masculine and the feminine, and deal with it most precisely.

Firstly, there is the doctrine of *Sat-Chit-Ânanda*:

Sat	Being	OBJECT
|	|	|
Chit	Consciousness	SUBJECT
|	|	|
Ânanda	Bliss	UNION

The simplest example of the relationship expressed here is as follows: a glass of water is *sat*; my thirst is *chit*; and my drinking of the glass of water is *ânanda*! In like manner, it is easy to see that *Sat-Chit-Ananda* is also the basis of erotic symbolism: the beloved is *sat*; the lover is *chit*; and the love that unites them is *ânanda*.

Secondly, there is the polarization known in Hinduism as *Purusha* and *Prakriti*, and in Medieval scholasticism as "Essence" (active, masculine, or "father") and "Substance" (passive, feminine, or "mother"):

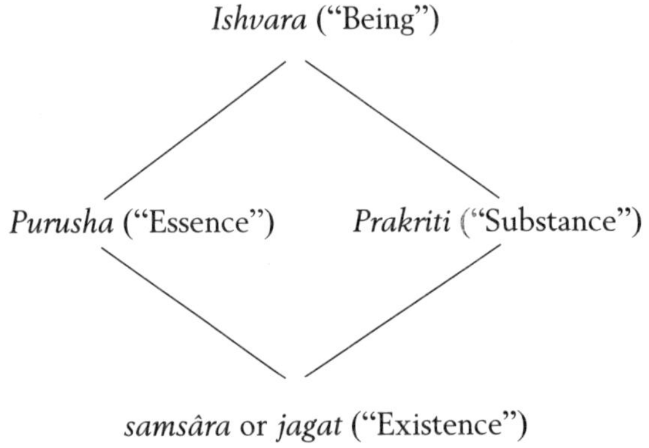

In Christian terms, this can be viewed as follows:

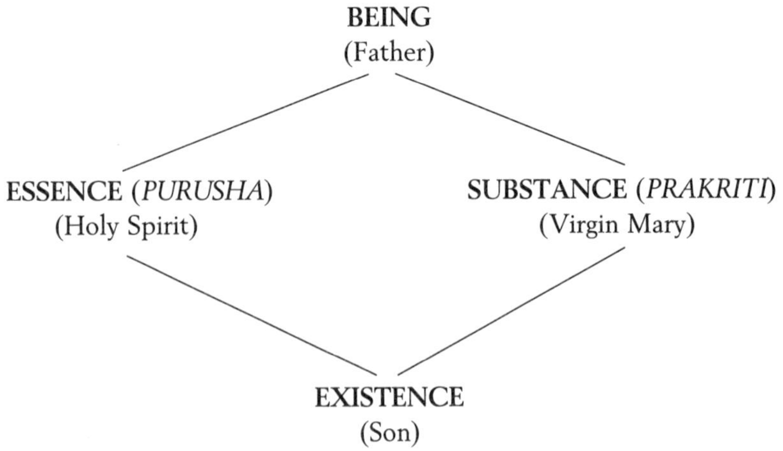

Thirdly—of relevance here as in other contexts—there is the doctrine of the three *gunas* (the "cosmic qualities" or "tendencies" in Hindu cosmology):

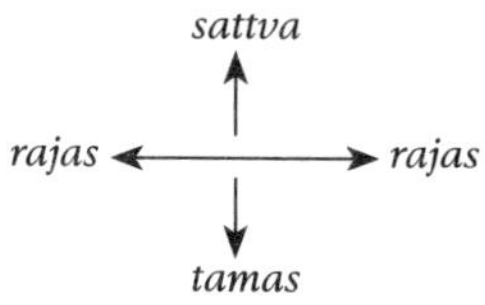

sattva = upward (or luminous) tendency

rajas = horizontal, expansive (or igneous) tendency

tamas = downward (opaque or heavy) tendency

The three *gunas* make their appearance when principles enter manifestation. Principles (i.e. supra-formal archetypes, prototypes, or essences) are incorruptible, but their various planes of manifestation are subject to corruption.

Manifestations of the masculine and feminine principles, when deviated, subverted, or "abnormal", do not translate or "symbolize" these principles as perfectly as do manifestations which are incorrupt or "normal". Corrupt manifestations are pathological; it is only what is healthy that represents the norm. Only incorrupt manifestations of the masculine and the feminine allow us to perceive their true nature. It therefore behooves us to strive to "see through" all corruptions of both principles in order to reach the (in fact divine and liberating) principles in themselves. This is the very definition of the spiritual Way. *Fiat mihi secundum verbum tuum.* ("Be it done unto me according to thy word.")

*
* *

The doctrine relating to *Purusha* and *Prakriti* is most fully developed and exploited by the perspective and practice known as *tantra*, and it is this which perhaps throws the maximum light on the nature and role of the masculine and the feminine:

The Two Poles of Universal Manifestation: "Essence" and "Substance" (*Purusha* and *Prakriti* or *Yang* and *Yin* in their two modes)

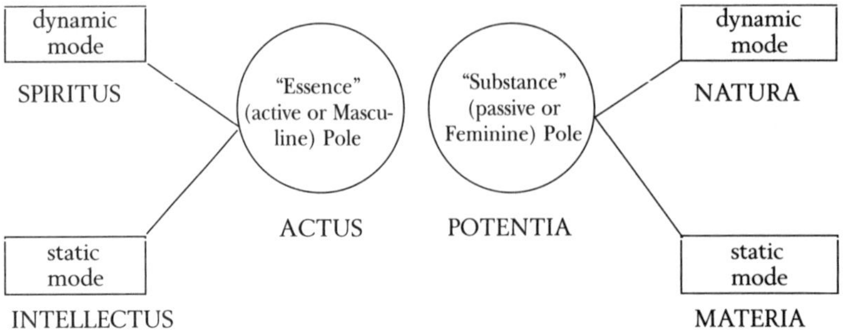

This presentation also indicates meanings of the pairs passive/active and static/dynamic as well as the metaphysical basis of the relationship between the sexes.

In *tantra*, it is characteristically a question of the union of the dynamic mode of the Passive Pole (NATURA) with the static mode of the Active Pole (INTELLECTUS). At the same time, of course, there is also a union of the dynamic mode of the Active Pole (SPIRITUS) with the static mode of the Passive Pole (MATERIA). It is the combination of the "unlikes", not of the "likes", that creates the indestructible bond.

> *Intellectus* stabilizes *Natura*; *Natura* vivifies *Intellectus*.
> *Spiritus* informs *Materia*; *Materia* captures *Spiritus*.[1]

*

* *

In the Taoist symbol of *Yin-Yang*, the active (or masculine) pole, *Yang*, is represented by a white field, but his static mode is represented by a black spot; the passive (or feminine) pole, *Yin*, is represented by a black field, but her dynamism is represented by a white spot. The intimacy of their union and the strength of their bond are represented in the symbol by the sinuous intertwining (so reminiscent of a tantric statue) of the two fields.

[1] See Frithjof Schuon, *Esoterism as Principle and as Way*, p. 39 and Titus Burckhardt, *Alchemy: Science of the Cosmos, Science of the Soul*, Chapter 9, "Nature can Overcome Nature".

Frithjof Schuon writes:

> Since *Yang* and *Yin* both derive from the *Tao*, they must inevitably reveal their underlying unity even on the plane of their divergence: this is shown by the symbol *Yin-Yang*, in which the black part contains a white spot, and inversely; this means that masculinity comprises an element of femininity, and femininity an element of masculinity. . . . Seen positively, the masculine refers to the Absolute, and the feminine to the Infinite; seen negatively, there is in masculinity a danger of contraction and hardening, while in femininity there is a danger of dissolving and indefinite exteriorization. . . . In geometrical symbolism, *Yang* is represented by surfaces which delimit and enclose (and thus maintain the link with unity), whereas *Yin* is represented by stars which project and radiate.[2]

*
* *

Titus Burckhardt says somewhere that man is hard outside and soft inside, whereas woman is soft outside and hard inside!

It is said traditionally that man's function is to command, and woman's function is to obey; however, it could perhaps also be said that it is man's function to command, and woman's function *not* to obey![3]

According to a popular humor in Muslim countries, it is man's function to make money, and woman's function to spend it!

*
* *

[2] *To Have a Center* (World Wisdom Books, Bloomington, Indiana, 1990), p. 86.

[3] Consider the wedding feast at Cana.

Let us end with a quotation from Frithjof Schuon's article on Shintoism. Having pointed out that, in Shinto mythology, it is the *left* eye of Izanagi that gives birth to the Sun and the *right* eye to the Moon (one might have expected the opposite), he goes on as follows:

> If, in the Japanese myth, it is the left eye which, contrary to expectation, gives birth to the Sun, this is because the Sun is here envisaged—as in the Germanic languages—under an aspect of femininity, of which it will then represent, not its passive and fragmentary side but, on the contrary, its active and maternal side: the Sun possesses fecundity, it is active in "creating" children, whereas the Moon—male according to a matriarchal perspective—is "sterile", in the sense that it knows not maternity, which alone is a "radiation"; the lunar male wanes in its fruitless solitude, obtaining expansion only thanks to woman who, in giving him joy, confers upon him as it were a life-giving light.[4]

Part II

God is above and beyond sex: He is neither masculine nor feminine. He possess both attributes in their plenitude, and is the essence or source of both. When, however, He first polarizes Himself, one speaks of Absolute and Infinite, *Purusha* and *Prakriti*, essence and substance, masculine and feminine, truth and beauty—that is to say, the Absolute or the masculine is mentioned first, and the Infinite or the feminine is mentioned second. One does not say Infinite and Absolute, *Prakriti* and *Purusha*, and so on.

The Infinite emerges from the Absolute as do rays from a point of light. This would suggest that the feminine emerges from the masculine, or is an aspect of the masculine. In Biblical language, Eve was created from Adam's rib.

It is of course fundamental that the masculine and the feminine are distinct, and have different roles. In cosmogony and cosmology, the masculine is the "warp" (vertical), the feminine is the "weft" (horizontal). This distinction is reflected, directly or indirectly, at all levels of manifestation. It is the basis of "Divine Art" and human art.

4 *Treasures of Buddhism* (World Wisdom Books, Bloomington, Indiana, 1993), p. 195.

*

*   *

There is direct analogy and indirect analogy.

As an example of indirect analogy, we may note that beauty ("feminine") is outward on earth, but inward in God. "Verily My Mercy precedeth my Wrath." There is also, however, direct analogy: truth ("masculine") is the prime attribute or quality of both God and man. "God is Truth." "Ye shall know the truth, and the truth shall make you free." Here the analogy is direct.

One might wish to paraphrase these words, and say: "Ye shall know beauty, and beauty shall make you free." This may well be so and, to the extent that it is, it is because beauty is the *shakti* ("efficient energy") of truth. In the words of Plato: "Beauty is the splendor of the Truth." Nevertheless, the formulation "beauty saves" is more "operative" rather than doctrinal, more mystical than metaphysical: it is a case of indirect analogy.

The doctrine that "truth saves" is one of direct analogy: it is both exoteric and esoteric, it is universal. In the present age, all religions (as long as they have not been falsified) still teach the truth, even if only from their respective exoteric points of view. However, I think it true to say that not one of them teaches beauty. They do so implicitly, of course, in their still extant sacred art. They also teach morality, which is a particular form of beauty (morality, in its essence, being truly described as "inward beauty"), but they do not teach beauty in the ordinary sense of the word. The emphasis on beauty as an integral part of the spiritual way is, in the present day, unique to Frithjof Schuon.

*

*   *

In the invocations *Jesu-Maria* and *Christe eleison*, the masculine element comes first, and the feminine element second. In the invocations *Sîtâ-Râm* and *Râdhâ-Krishna*, the feminine element comes first, certainly with an "operative" intent, and no doubt also because of Hinduism's love of femininity, and its awareness of the transforming and "tantric" role of what Frithjof Schuon calls "higher *Mâyâ*".

*

*   *

God is the Absolute and the Infinite. There can be both complementarity and inequality between the two Divine Attributes. In the saying: "Beauty is the splendor of the Truth, and Truth is the essence of Beauty", the masculine is greater than the feminine. When one talks of "Justice" and "Mercy", the feminine is greater than the masculine. Which is the greater between mathematics and music? Both are inherent in reality.

Between man and woman, there are three relationships: two of "hierarchy", and one of "complementarity". As regards the first hierarchical relationship, man is superior, functionally, socially, etc.

In the second hierarchical relationship, which is "tantric" or mystical, woman may be regarded as superior. Frithjof Schuon writes as follows: "Even though, *a priori*, femininity is subordinate to virility (since the latter refers to the Principle and the former to Manifestation), it also comprises an aspect which makes it superior to a certain aspect of the masculine pole; for the Divine Principle has an aspect of unlimitedness . . . which takes precedence over a certain more relative aspect of determination. . . ."[5]

As regards the third relationship, that of "complementarity", this is expressed by the fundamental and universal symbol of *Yin-Yang*. Man possesses a feminine aspect and woman possesses a masculine aspect, since each is a human being. Frithjof Schuon writes beautifully:

> *Nichts rührt den Mann wie Schönheit und Unschuld, deshalb liebt er das Weib. Nichts erfüllt das Weib wie Geist und Kraft, deshalb liebt es den Mann.*
>
> "Nothing stirs man like beauty and innocence, therefore he loves woman. Nothing fulfills woman like intellect and strength, therefore she loves man."[6]

According to the principle of *Yin-Yang*, man should (in the appropriate fashion) possess beauty and innocence, and woman (in the appropriate fashion) should possess intellect and strength.

*

* *

[5] *From the Divine to the Human* (World Wisdom Books, Bloomington, Indiana, 1982), pp. 94-95.

[6] *Leitgedanken zur Urbesinnung* ("Themes for Meditation") (Zürich, 1935), p. 44.

All Holy Scriptures refer to God in the masculine. This is because the masculine, by its nature, represents totality. The feminine does not. It represents a quality or attribute of totality.

Both theologically and metaphysically, both exoterically and esoterically, God is "masculine" (in Arabic *Hûwa* = He), that is to say, the masculine is taken as the symbol of totality. For this reason, in spirituality, the soul (*anima*) is often regarded as feminine in relation to the Spirit (*Spiritus* = *Intellectus* = *Animus*).

Mystically or operatively, however, God, or the Divine Essence, may be conceived as "feminine" (in Arabic *Hîya* = She), but this is "mystical" or "tantric", and is not universal. Here, it is the spiritual aspirant who is "masculine". This rather special symbolic representation is obviously not appropriate in the case of female spiritual aspirants. One cannot imagine it being used by St. Catherine of Siena, or St. Theresa of Ávila! The view of the Divine Essence as "feminine" therefore does not constitute a universal or normative doctrine.

13. THE ROLE OF CULTURE IN EDUCATION

The spiritual life has been described as the "interiorization of the outward" (*khalwa*) and the "exteriorization of the inward" (*jalwa*).[1] Education is an aspect of the latter process; the very etymology of the word (*e-ducare*, "to lead out") is an indication of this. As a "leading-out", education is a rendering explicit of the immanent Intellect (*Intellectus* or *Nous*), the seat of which, symbolically speaking, is the heart. As Frithjof Schuon has said more than once: "The Intellect can know everything that is knowable." This is because "heart-knowledge" (*gnosis*) is innate, and thus already fully present within us, in a state of virtuality.[2] This virtuality has to be realized, and this realization is education. This corresponds to the Platonic doctrine of "recollection" (*anamnesis*), which in the last analysis is the "remembrance of God" (*memoria Dei*). "The Kingdom of Heaven is within you."

Man is constituted by the ternary: Spirit, soul, and body (*Spiritus, anima, corpus*); only the last two are exclusively individual or human, the first being supra-individual or universal. The Intellect (*Intellectus*) is identifiable with the Spirit: Intellect and Spirit are but two sides of the same coin, the former pertaining to the theoretical or doctrinal and the latter to the practical or realizational. They pertain respectively to the objective (or discriminatory) and the subjective (or unitive) modes of knowing.

It is easy to see how education, both etymologically and philosophically, is an "exteriorization of the inward". But it is also an "interiorization of the outward", for an important function of education is precisely to ensure that the myriad of impressions coming from the outside be "inwardly digested" and reduced to unity. Thus education is both "exteriorization of the inward" (intellectuality) and "interiorization of the outward" (spirituality). It is both *jalwa* and *khalwa*.

The following summary of terminology may be useful:

[1] These "alchemical" definitions come from Frithjof Schuon. In Arabic, *khalwa* means "spiritual retreat" and *jalwa* means "spiritual radiance", the former being logically prior to the latter. The two processes are symbolized respectively by the colors black and gold.

[2] Examples (immediately apparent, and built into the human substance) of this innate and objective knowledge are our sense of logic, our capacity for arithmetic, our sense of justice, and our sense of right and wrong.

English	Latin	Greek	Arabic
Spirit (Intellect)	*Spiritus* (*Intellectus*)	*Pneuma* (*Nous*)	*Rûh* (*'Aql*)
soul	*anima*	*psyche*	*nafs*
body	*corpus*	*soma*	*jism*

In modern parlance, "intellectual" is often wrongly taken as a synonym of "mental" or "rational". In fact, unlike the Intellect, which is "above" the soul, the mind or the reason is a content of the soul, as are the other human faculties: will, affect or sentiment, imagination, and memory. The spiritual or intellectual faculty, on the other hand—because of its higher level—can be categorized as "angelic". The operation of the Intellect is referred to as "intellectual intuition" or "intellection". (*For the contents of the soul, see the second table on p. 46.*)

This is not to say that there is an absolute barrier between Intellect and mind. The Intellect may be compared to the center of a circle, and the mind to the circumference. Metaphorically speaking, the Greek philosophers and the Medieval Schoolmen were concerned with the "center" or, to put it even more accurately, with the Transcendent, symbolized by the axis running vertically through it. The Transcendent element—man's infinitely precious link with the higher levels of Reality (*see the explanatory table on p. 49*)—is accessible only through faith, the voice of conscience, or what might be called Platonic intuition or "intellection". From the Renaissance onwards such a vision of the higher levels of Reality became increasingly ignored, and latterly was dismissed as mere "dogma" or "superstition". Properly modern philosophy—the starting-point of which was no longer certainty, but doubt—was epitomized by the 17th century philosophers Descartes and Kant and, from their time until now has, with a few honorable exceptions, been subject to a continuing downhill process.

In the light of the foregoing, we are also able to see that the error, in a nutshell, of psychologists such as Jung, is completely to confuse Spirit and soul and so, in the last analysis, entirely to "abolish" Spirit (the only truly supra-individual, "archetypal", or "objective" element in man). It is not difficult to see the chaos—and the damage—that results from this fatal and anti-Platonic act of blindness.

The linking of education with spirituality may cause some surprise; but the parable of the talents applies to the mind as well as to every other faculty. "Thou shalt love the Lord thy God with all thy heart and with all thy soul . . . and *with all thy mind.* It is at our peril that we neglect the need for "a well-stocked mind";[3] for it is surely obvious that, from a purely spiritual point of view, the mind cannot be allowed to lie fallow. This would allow it to become a playground for the devil, and *si monumentum requiris, circumspice* ("if you seek proof, just look around").

Use of the phrase "a well-stocked mind" makes it necessary immediately to specify (and never more so than in the "reign of quantity" that is the present age) that, as far as true education is concerned, it is nevertheless a question, not of quantity (however intoxicating), but of quality; not of shadows (however beguiling), but of substance; not of trivia (however intriguing), but of essentials. In the present age, more than in all previous ages, the grasping of a true and permanent principle is infinitely more precious than the piling up of a hundred undigested and un-understood contingencies. In addition, there is no greater joy.

Since education, by definition, is a thing of the *mind*, we can do no better than cite here the injunction of St. Paul:

> Whatsoever things are true, whatsoever things are honest, whatsoever things are just, whatsoever things are pure, whatsoever things are lovely, whatsoever things are of good report; if there be any virtue, and if there be any praise, *think* on these things. (*Philippians*, 4, 8)

One might say: whatsoever things are true, good, and beautiful; or whatsoever things manifest or reflect the Absolute, the Infinite, and the Perfect.

*

* *

All civilizations—for example, the Chinese, Hindu, Greco-Roman, Christian, and Islamic—manifest the central or cardinal role of learning, at least for those classes or individuals capable of it. In this connection, it might be objected that the North American Indians—who possessed a daunting spiritual tradition if ever there was one—were not educated. In the light of the considerations expressed above, however, it is clear that the Red Indians too, in their own fashion, were "educated". To regard the Indians as uneducated because they were un-

[3] "My people are destroyed for lack of knowledge" (*Hosea*, 4, 6). The text goes on: "Because thou hast rejected knowledge, I will also reject thee".

lettered, would be like regarding the Buddhists as atheistic, because they envisage Ultimate Reality as a supreme State (*Nirvâna* or *Bodhi*) rather than as a supreme Being. Just as the Buddhists are manifestly different from the superficial and arrogant atheists of modern times, so the Indians are manifestly different from the technologically-trained but culturally-uneducated and mentally-immature people of modern times. The Indians' Book is Nature herself, and none have ever known this book better.

Education has many forms and, in any case, has in view only those classes and individuals who are capable of receiving it. Indeed the type of literacy resulting from the leveling-downward "universal" education of the last hundred years may even be inimical to culture, as Ananda Coomaraswamy has so trenchantly pointed out in his important essay "The Bugbear of Literacy". Coomaraswamy demonstrates beyond any dispute how the new-found capacity of the immature mind to read modern printed material—now always to hand in such staggering quantity[4]—has killed the rich traditional culture (largely oral for the mass of the people) in many societies, including European ones. This is the opposite of true education, which is depth, subtlety, and finally, wisdom.

*

* *

The European tradition consists of two currents: the Greek and the Christian, or the Classical and the Medieval. The Greek current is evoked by such names as Homer, Pythagoras, and Plato; the Christian current is evoked not only by such figures as St. Gregory Palamas and Meister Eckhart ("apophatic" and "gnostic" metaphysicians respectively), but also by St. Augustine and St. Thomas Aquinas (whose viewpoints represent two important strands, amongst others, of Western Christian thought). Christianity is also epitomized by that "second Christ" (*alter Christus*), St. Francis of Assisi, and by the great epic poet of Christendom, Dante Alighieri. In practical terms, education in Europe has obviously to take account of both the Classical and the Medieval currents.

[4] As Lord Northbourne has said (referring to the industrialized countries): "We live in an age of plenty; but what use is plenty of rubbish?" (*Look to the Land*, London, Dent, 1940, Sophia Perennis, Hillsdale, NY, 2003).

In English-speaking countries, a good education must start with the Christian catechism and attendance at Divine Worship, as well as the study of the Bible and the most celebrated Christian authors, such as the great names just mentioned. It must include the study of Greek and Latin, coupled with some Homer, Plato, Virgil, Horace, Cicero and other ancient authors. The "history of philosophy" (an understanding of the relative "stability" of Ancient and Medieval philosophy as contrasted with the innovative nature and "instability" of Modern philosophy[5]) is obviously necessary. Likewise, some notion of the "philosophy of science"—especially as regards the differing conceptions of science on the part of Ancient and Medieval times on the one hand and Modern times on the other—is also desirable. In present circumstances, some *Religionswissenschaft* or "comparative religion" is no doubt essential, but this must be of high quality and taught from a conservative and believing point of view, which, while being respectful of the authenticity of the non-Christian religions, is not lethal to the student's faith in his own religion.

An important branch of education—and one which should never be forgotten—is what might be called "art appreciation" or "history of art". This refers above all to the ability to discriminate between "traditional" art (that is, Medieval and Oriental) and "non-traditional" art (that is, European art of the Renaissance and post-Renaissance periods). Also, at a much more outward—but still very important—level, one must discriminate between art that is still "human", however superficial and sentimental it may be, and the "infra-human" or satanic art of modern times.[6]

Also essential are subjects such as English and European (and perhaps world) history and literature—within the limits of the reasonable and the possible. It should be stressed that this proviso applies throughout, as does also the frequently forgotten principle that formal or "scholastic" education is only intended for those fit to profit by it. The need for the study of modern languages, above all French and German, is apparent. A study of these two languages, coupled with the study of Greek and Latin, has the additional merit of facili-

[5] Frithjof Schuon has pointed out that, whereas Greek and Medieval philosophy is founded on certainty, the philosophy of Descartes, Kant, and their successors is founded on doubt.

[6] Regarding the successive, downward-cascading, phases of post-Medieval art, see the last chapter of the invaluable treatise *Sacred Art in East and West* by Titus Burckhardt.

tating access to other modern European languages, such as Italian and Spanish. Obviously all aspects of mathematics must be available, and the essentials taught to all.

In the modern situation, modern science and technology are inescapable, since, in some branch or other, they will be indispensable for most, from the point of view of earning a livelihood. Modern science and technology, however, are alien to culture and consequently do not pertain to education as defined in this chapter.

III.

Remembering (*practice*)

"Remember God with much remembrance."

Koran, 33, 41

14. WHAT IS MYSTICISM?

Except by those who reject it or are ignorant of it entirely, it is generally understood that mysticism claims to be concerned with "Ultimate Reality". The relationship in question is mostly taken to be of an "experiential" kind, and the phrase "mystical experience" is often used—the assumed object of the experience being, precisely, "Ultimate Reality", which is allegedly transcendent and hidden in regard to our ordinary senses. This mystical experience is held to be "incommunicable" and, particularly when doubt is cast on the alleged object of the experience, it is often said to be, in a pejorative sense, purely subjective.

Nevertheless, it would generally be admitted that, as well as "mystical experience", there is also "mystical doctrine". There is thus at least something that can be communicated (for this is what doctrine means), and at the same time something that is "objective", for whatever can be transmitted must needs be objective, even should the object in question prove to be illusory. The subjective as such cannot be transmitted,[1] but its object can—at least in conceptual terms. To say: "I have experienced something indescribable and incommunicable" is already a description and a communication. As such it can be considered objectively by a third party and, depending on the adequacy of the description, the sensitivity of the hearer, and the reality of the object, it can even stir within him a responsive chord. This means that in favorable circumstances it can, to a greater or lesser degree, stimulate in the hearer a similar intuition or "experience".

The assumed object of both "mystical experience" and "mystical doctrine" is Ultimate Reality. Mystical doctrine may call this the One, the Absolute, the Infinite, the Supreme Self, the Supreme Being, or some other name, and mystical experience is deemed to be union therewith, to whatever degree and in whatever mode. With this end in view, one also speaks of the "mystical way" or the "mystical path". This is the process of "unification" with the One, the Supreme Self,

[1] In modern subjectivism, what is expressed is only a subject that is already relative, namely the passional, sentimental, and imaginative ego; in order to express itself, it necessarily makes use of objective elements which it chooses arbitrarily, while separating itself arrogantly and foolishly from objective reality. The "purely subjective", in the modern world, can only announce its presence by gasps and howls, and this is the very definition of modern "avant-garde" poetry.

or the Supreme Being—all of these being names given to Ultimate Reality.

From all of this, it clearly emerges that mysticism or mystical experience has two poles, namely mystical doctrine and the mystical way or path. Thus in mysticism, as in other spheres, it is a question of doctrine and method, or theory and practice. These twin elements of mysticism will be examined in detail in the course of this essay. The validity and justifiability of mysticism, let it be said right away, depend on the validity and justifiability of its object. If this be a reality, the experience is valid and, in the manner described, capable of being communicated to, and evoked in, a third party.

*

* *

As is often done, I have spoken of mysticism in a manner that might give the impression that mysticism is an independent entity capable of existing in a vacuum. Such an impression would be false, however, since in practice mysticism only makes its appearance within the framework of one or other of the revealed religions. Indeed it would be true to say that mysticism constitutes the inward or spiritual dimension of every religion. Mysticism is esoterism, while the outward religious framework is the respective exoterism. The exoterism is for all, but the corresponding esoterism is only for those who feel a call thereto. Esoterism, unlike exoterism, cannot be imposed. It is strictly a matter of vocation.

It has been said that "all paths lead to the same summit". In this symbol, the variety of religions is represented by the multiplicity of starting-points around the circumferential base of a cone or mountain. The radial, upward, pathways are the mystical paths. The oneness of mysticism is a reality only at the point that is the summit. The pathways are many, but their goal is one. As they approach this goal, the various pathways more and more resemble one another, but only at the Summit do they coincide. Until then, in spite of resemblances and analogies, they remain separate, and indeed each path is imbued with a distinctive perfume or color—Islamic mysticism is clearly not Christian mysticism—but at the Summit these various colors are (still speaking symbolically) reintegrated into the uncolored Light. Islamic mysticism and Christian mysticism are one only in God.

It is this point of "uncolored Light", where the different religions come together, that is the basis of the *philosophia perennis* or *religio perennis*. This is the supra-formal, divine truth which is the source of each religion, and which each religion incorporates. The heart of each exoterism is its corresponding esoterism, and the heart of each esoterism is the *religio perennis*—or esoterism in the pure state.

In all the religions, the goal of mysticism is God, who may also be given such names as the One, the Absolute, the Infinite, the Supreme Self, the Supreme Being.[2] In sapiential or "theosophic" mysticism, the goal is said to be the Truth, conceived as a living Reality capable of being experienced. Mysticism thus has three components: the doctrine concerning God or Ultimate Reality ("mystical doctrine"), "oneness" with God or Ultimate Reality ("mystical experience"), and the movement that leads from the former to the latter ("the mystical path"). In other words: the doctrine of Unity, the experience of Union, and the path of Unification.

Mystical doctrine is one and the same as metaphysics or mystical theology. Mystical experience, when present in a total or at least sufficient degree, is salvation or liberation. And the purpose of the mystical path is "spiritual realization", i.e., the progression from outward to inward, from belief to vision, or (in Scholastic terms) from Potency to Act.

*

* *

Many people are familiar with the three fundamental modes of spiritual realization proclaimed by Hinduism: *karma-mârga* (the "Way of Action"), *bhakti-mârga* (the "Way of Love"), and *jñâna-mârga* (the "Way of Knowledge"). These correspond to the three degrees or dimensions of Sufism: *makhâfa* ("Fear"), *mahabba* ("Love"), and *ma'rifa* ("Knowledge" or "Gnosis").[3]

Strictly speaking, it is only *bhakti* and *jñâna* (i.e. *mahabba* and *ma'rifa*) that constitute mysticism: mysticism is either a way of Love, a way of Knowledge, or a combination of both. One will recall the

[2] This also includes the "non-theistic" religion of Buddhism, since here too Ultimate Reality, variously referred to in different contexts as *Dharma* ("Law"), *Âtmâ* ("Self"), *Nirvâna* ("Extinction"), or *Bodhi* ("Knowledge"), is seen as transcendent and absolute.

[3] This word is used purely etymologically, and does not hark back to the current, in the early history of Christianity, known as "gnosticism". "Gnosis", from the Greek, is the only adequate English rendering for the Sanskrit *jñâna* (with which in fact it is cognate) and the Arabic *ma'rifa*.

occasion in the life of Christ when he was received in the house of the sisters Martha and Mary. What has come to be known in Christianity as the "Way of Martha" is paralleled by the Hindu *karma-mârga*, the way of religious observance and good works. The contemplative or mystical way, on the other hand, is the "Way of Mary", which comprises two modes, namely, *bhakti-mârga* (the "Way of Love") and *jñâna-mârga* (the "Way of Knowledge"). *Karma* as such is purely exoteric, but it is important to stress that there is always a karmic component within both *bhakti* and *jñâna*. The Way of Love and the Way of Knowledge both necessarily contain an element of Fear or conformity. Likewise, the Way of Knowledge invariably contains within it the reality of Love. As for the Way of Love, which is composed of faith and devotion, it contains an indirect element of *jñâna* in the form of dogmatic and speculative theology. This element lies in the intellectual speculation as such, not in its object, the latter being limited by definition,[4] failing which it would not be a question of *bhakti*, but of *jñâna*. In spite of the presence in each Way of elements of the two others, the three Ways *karma*, *bhakti*, and *jñâna* (or *makhâfa*, *mahabba*, and *ma'rifa*) represent three specific and easily distinguishable modes of religious aspiration.

As for the question as to which of these paths a given devotee adheres to, it is overwhelmingly a matter of temperament and vocation. It is a case where the Way chooses the individual and not the individual the Way.

Historically speaking, Christian mysticism has been characterized in the main by the "Way of Love", whereas Hindu mysticism and Islamic mysticism comprise both the "Way of Love" and the "Way of Knowledge". The language of the "Way of Love" has a remarkably similar ring in whichever mysticism it crops up, but the more jñânic formulations of Hinduism and the more "gnostic" formulations of Sufism tend to strike a foreign note in the ears of those who are familiar only with Christian, or at any rate bhaktic, forms of spirituality.[5]

[4] In the "Way of Love" (*bhakti* or *mahabba*), God is envisaged at the level of "Being" (which has as consequence that the Lord and the worshiper always remain distinct). In the Way of Knowledge (*jñâna* or *ma'rifa*), on the other hand, God is envisaged at the level of "Beyond-Being" or "Essence".

[5] Those who, by way of exception, have manifested the "Way of Knowledge" in Christianity include such great figures as Dionysius the Areopagite, Meister Eckhart, Albertus Magnus, and Angelus Silesius. It is precisely the works of *jñânins* such as these that have tended to cause ripples in the generally bhaktic climate of Christianity.

*
* *

The goal of religion, in all its varieties, is salvation. What, then, is the difference between exoterism and esoterism? Exoterism is formalistic, but faith and devotion can give it depth. Esoterism is "deep"—supra-formal—by definition, and is the apanage only of those with the relevant vocation. Here forms are transcended, in that they are seen as symbolic expressions of the essence. In esoterism too faith is essential, but here it has the meaning of sincerity and total commitment—effort towards "realization". It means the acquisition of the essential virtues of humility and charity, and the opening of the soul to Divine grace. Metaphysically, the difference between exoterism and esoterism, or between formalism and supra-formalism, lies in how the final Goal is envisaged: in exoterism (and in esoterism of the "bhaktic" type), God is envisaged at the level of "Being" (the Creator and the Judge): no matter how deep, how sublime, the exoterist's fervor, Lord and worshiper always remain distinct. In "jñânic" esoterism, on the other hand, God is envisaged at the level of "Beyond-Being" (the Divine Essence). At this level, it is perceived that Lord and worshiper (the latter known to be created in the image of the former) share a common essence, and this opens up the possibility of ultimate Divine Union.

*
* *

Reference was made earlier to "subjective" and "objective", and it may be useful to indicate precisely whence these two concepts derive. The most direct key in this regard is the Hindu appellation for the Divinity: *Sat-Chit-Ânanda.* This expression is usually translated as "Being-Consciousness-Bliss". This is accurate, and enables one to see that "Being" is the Divine Object (God Transcendent or Ultimate Reality), "Consciousness" is the Divine Subject (God Immanent or the Supreme Self), while "Bliss"—the harmonious coming-together of the two—is Divine Union. The most fundamental translation therefore of *Sat-Chit-Ânanda* is "Object-Subject-Union". This is the model, or origin, of all possible objects and subjects, and of the longing of the latter for the former.[6]

[6] *Sat-Chit-Ânanda* may also be interpreted as "Known-Knower-Knowledge" or "Beloved-Lover-Love".

This trinitarian aspect of the Divinity is universal, and is found in all religions. In Christianity it is the central dogma: God the Father, God the Son, and God the Holy Spirit. The analogy between the Christian Trinity and "Being-Consciousness-Bliss" can be seen from certain doctrinal expositions of the Greek Fathers and also from St. Augustine's designation of the Christian Trinity as "Being-Wisdom-Life". In Islam, although it is above all the religion of strict monotheism, certain Sufi formulations evoke the selfsame trinitarian aspect of the Divinity. Reference will be made later to the question of spiritual realization, but in Sufism this is essentially mediated by the invocation (*dhikr*) of the Name of God. In this connection it is said that God is not only That which is invoked (*Madhkûr*), but also That within us which invokes (*Dhâkir*), and even the invocation itself, since, in the last analysis, this is none other than the internal Act (*Dhikr*) of God.[7] We thus have the ternary *Madhkûr-Dhâkir-Dhikr* ("Invoked-Invoker-Invocation"), which is yet another form of the basic ternary "Object-Subject-Union". This cardinal relationship is the very essence of the theory and practice of mysticism, for this "Union" *in divinis* is the prefiguration of and pattern for the union of man with God.[8] Hindu, Christian, and Sufi doctrine coincide in elucidating just why this is so.

*

*　*

One of the most significant characteristics of mystical doctrine stemming from several of the great religions—and made explicit, for example, in the treatises of jñânic or gnostic mystics such as Shankara, Eckhart, and Ibn 'Arabî—is the distinction made, within God Himself, between God and the Godhead, between "Being" and "Essence", or between "Being" and "Beyond-Being".[9] In ordinary theological doctrine, the fundamental distinction is between God and man, or between the Uncreated and the created. Mystical or esoteric doctrine, on the other hand, makes a distinction within each of these two terms. Thus, within the Uncreated (viewed as the "Divine Essence" or "Beyond-Being"), there is already a *prefiguration* of creation, and

[7] That this Divine Act should pass through man is the mystery of salvation.

[8] It will easily be seen that it is also the prefiguration of every other union under the sun, for example, conjugal union.

[9] The same distinction is also made by St. Gregory Palamas in his doctrine of the Divine Essence and the Divine Energies.

this is God as "Being". "Beyond-Being" is the principle of "Being", and God as Being (the immediate Creator of the world) is the principle of existence or creation.

Within creation—itself relative—there is also a distinction to be made, for within creation there is a *reflection* of the Uncreated (the Absolute) in the form of Truth and Virtue, Symbol and Sacrament, Prophet or Redeemer. Once again mystical doctrine renders explicit the reality of mystical union, for it is by uniting himself with the "created" Symbol or Sacrament (for example, in truth, in beauty,[10] in virtue, in the Eucharist, or in the Invocation of a Divine Name), that the mystic realizes his union with (or reintegration into) the uncreated Divinity. Only through the sacramental perfecting of the created, can one reach the Uncreated. This is what is meant in Christianity by "the imitation of Christ", or in Islam by the observance of the *Sunna* (the Wont of the Prophet Mohammed).

This exposition is taken from the writings of Frithjof Schuon,[11] who has explained how "Being" (the *prefiguration* of the relative in the Absolute) is the uncreated Logos, whereas the *reflection* of the Absolute in the relative (namely: truth, beauty, virtue, Prophet, Savior) is the created Logos. Without this "bridge" (the Logos with its created and uncreated aspects), no contact whatsoever between created and Uncreated, between man and God, would be possible:[12] the gulf between the two would be unbridgeable. This would be "dualism", not "Non-Dualism" (or *Advaita*, to use the term from Shankaran metaphysics), and the very opposite of mysticism.

For a summary, in diagrammatic form, of the doctrine of the Logos, and its cardinal relevance to the mystical path, please see the table on p. 59.

Within each religion, the Founder is the personification of the Logos, and his role as such is always made explicit. Christ said: "No man cometh to the Father but by me." The Prophet Mohammed said: "He that hath seen me, hath seen God." The Buddha said: "He who

[10] "Virtue is inward beauty, and beauty is outward virtue". The liberating, or inwardly transforming, power of beauty, be it of virgin nature or of traditional art, can play a profound role in the spiritual life. (*See p. 73, 3rd paragraph and p. 81, 2nd paragraph.*)

[11] See especially *Esoterism as Principle and as Way.*

[12] The error of deism is precisely that it has no concept of the role of the Logos and envisages no such bridge.

sees the *Dharma* sees me, and he who sees me sees the *Dharma*." Mystical union is realized only through the Logos.

This brings us directly to the three classical "stages" (*maqâmât* in Arabic) recognized by all mysticisms:

I. Purification (or Purgation),
II. Perfection (or Illumination),
III. Union.

The second stage, "Perfection", corresponds precisely to the aspirant's assimilation to the created Logos. In Christianity, this takes the form of the "imitation of Christ" and in Islam, the observance—inward and symbolically total—of the "Wont of the Prophet" (*Sunna*). Prayers such as the "Hail Mary" (*Ave Maria*) in Catholicism and the "Blessing on the Prophet" (*salât 'alâ 'n-Nabî*) in Islam, which contain the names of the created Logos (*Jesus* and *Muhammad* respectively), are instrumental to the end in view.

*
* *

As we have seen, mysticism includes both mystical doctrine and mystical experience. Mystical experience is the inward and unitive "realization" of the doctrine. This is the domain of spiritual method. In Hinduism spiritual method is represented by *yoga*—not the physical exercises derived from *hatha-yoga* now widely experimented with in the West, but *raja-yoga*, the "royal art" of contemplation and union. If, in Hinduism, the *veda* (knowledge) is the *scientia sacra*, then *yoga* (union) is the corresponding *ars sacra* or *operatio sacra*. Here the saying of the Medieval French architect Jean Mignot applies with fullest force: *ars sine scientiâ nihil.* One cannot meaningfully or effectively practice anything, if one does not know what one is doing. Above all, one cannot practice a spiritual method except on the basis of previously comprehended spiritual doctrine which is both the motivation and the paradigm for the spiritual work to be undertaken. If doctrine without method is hypocrisy or sterility, then method without doctrine means going astray, and sometimes dangerously. This makes clear why doctrine must be "orthodox"—that is, in essential conformity with the subtle contours of truth. Here it must be noted that pseudo-doctrine, born of nothing more than human invention, is one of the most powerful causes of going astray.

These points have to be stressed, because in the present age many of those attracted by mysticism are eager at all costs for "experience"—without caring to ask themselves: experience of what—and without the safeguards either of conforming to the discipline of a religious tradition or of receiving permission and guidance from a spiritual authority. It is precisely this illegitimate wresting of method from doctrine that is harmful. The more real and effective the spiritual method appropriated, the more dangerous it can be for the appropriator. There are many recorded cases of psychological and spiritual damage resulting from the unauthorized use (i.e., the profanation) of religious rites and sacraments.

In the past, it was the opposite fault that was most likely: to know the truth, but—through weakness, passion, or pride—to fail to put it into practice; in other words, it was a question of hypocrisy, and not the heresy—most commonly in the shape of a "false sincerity"—characteristic of modern times. How typical of the age we live in that, here as elsewhere, it stands on its head! The new shortcoming is infinitely worse than the earlier one. It is forgotten that every "quest" inevitably has an object and, whether one cares to recall it or not, the object of a mystical or spiritual quest is Ultimate Reality or God. With such an object one cannot trifle with impunity.

Yoga is the way or method of union with God, through a dedicated concentration on Him. A particularly direct form of this is (in Hindu terms) *japa-yoga*, which involves the enduring invocation of a *mantra* (a Divine Name or a formula containing a Divine Name). *Mutatis mutandis*, this spiritual method plays a central role in all mysticisms. In *Mahâyâna* Buddhism, for example, it occurs in the form of the Tibetan *Mani* and the Japanese *Nembutsu*. In Islam, nothing is more enjoined on the spiritual aspirant than *dhikr Allâh*, the "remembrance of God" through the invocation of His Name. In Hesychasm (the mysticism of Eastern Christianity), invocation of the Divine Name takes the form of the "Prayer of Jesus", a practice vividly described in *The Way of a Russian Pilgrim*.[13] The analogous method in Western Christianity is the cult of the Holy Name. This flourished in the Middle Ages, and was also preached with poignancy and single-mindedness in the 15th century by St. Bernardino of Siena: "Everything that God has created for the salvation of the world is hidden in the Name of Jesus." The practice was revived, in the form of the invocation *Jesu-Maria*, in

[13] *The Way of a Pilgrim* (S.P.C.K., London, 1954).

the revelations made to Sister Consolata, an Italian Capuchin nun, in the earlier part of the 20th century.[14]

This method of concentrating on a revealed Divine Name indicates clearly that mysticism is the very opposite of giving free rein to man's unregenerate subjectivity. In fact, it is the exposing of his unregenerate subjectivity to the normative and transforming influence of the revealed Object, the Sacrament or Symbol of the religion in question. It was in this respect that St. Paul could say: "Not I, but Christ in me." At the same time, and even more esoterically, it is the exposing of our paltry egoism, seen in turn as an "object", to the withering and yet quickening influence of the divine Subject, the immanent Self.[15] This possibility is envisaged in Islam in the *hadîth qudsî* (a "Divine saying" through the mouth of the Prophet Mohammed): "I (God) am the hearing whereby he (the slave) heareth."[16] The vehicle of both processes is the Invocation of a Divine Name (which is both Subject and Object), within a strictly traditional and orthodox framework, and with the authorization of an authentic spiritual master. In this domain, there is no room for curiosity and experiment.

*

*   *

In the mysticisms of several religions, the soul's quest for God is symbolized in terms of the mutual longing of the lover and the beloved. St. John of the Cross, for example, makes use of this symbolism in his mystical poetry, from which the following verses are quoted:

Oh noche que guiaste
Oh noche amable más que el alborada:
Oh noche que juntaste
Amado con amada
Amada en el Amado transformada!

[14] *Jesus Appeals to the World* (Alba House [Society of St. Paul], Staten Island NY, 1971).

[15] This synthesis of the dual aspect of realization or method is taken from the writings of Frithjof Schuon. See especially *Eye of the Heart*, chapter "Microcosm and Symbol".

[16] A similar thought is echoed in the words of St. Theresa of Ávila: "Christ has no body now on earth but yours, no hands but yours, no feet but yours; yours are the eyes through which is to look out Christ's compassion on the world; yours are the feet on which he is to go about doing good, and yours are the hands with which he is to bless us now."

O night that led'st me thus!
O night more winsome than the rising sun!
O night that madest us,
Lover and lov'd as one,
Lover transformed in lov'd, love's journey done!
(translated by Professor E. Allison Peers)

Descubre tu presencia,
Y máteme tu vista y hermosura;
Mira que la dolencia
De amor que no se cura
Sino con la presencia y la figura.

Reveal your presence clearly
And kill me with the beauty you discover,
For pains acquired so dearly
From love, cannot recover
Save only through the presence of the lover.
(translated by Roy Campbell)

As a child of the 16th century, St. John of the Cross sought to convey his "subjective" experiences rather than objective doctrine, as the mystics of a few centuries earlier had done. And yet he never wavered from the Divine Object of all mystical striving. At the practical level, in an instruction for aspirants, he said, for example: "All goodness is a loan from God." The soul's subjectivity is uncertain; only the objective reality, that comes from beyond it, is absolutely certain.

*
* *

Mysticism was earlier defined as the inward or spiritual dimension contained within every religion—each religion being understood as a separate and specific Divine Revelation. Religion comprises a "periphery" and a "center", in other words, an exoterism and an esoterism. The exoterism is the providential expression or vehicle of the esoterism within it, and the esoterism is the supra-formal essence of the corresponding exoterism. This is why mysticism or esoterism—erroneously regarded by some as "unorthodox"—can in no way subvert the religious formalism of which it is the sap.

On the other hand, "essence" so far transcends "form", that inevitably it sometimes "breaks" it. Conflicts have at times occurred between the purest mysticism and the respective exoteric authority; the cases of Meister Eckhart in medieval Christendom and Al-Hallâj in Islam—the one leading to condemnation and the other to martyrdom—provide striking examples. Nevertheless Eckhart enunciated this shattering of forms in a positive way when he said: "If thou wouldst reach the kernel, thou must break the shell." It is hardly necessary to add that such a "transcending" of forms is at the very antipodes of heresy, which is a crude violation of the forms of a religion at their own level. Forms can be transcended only "from above" (or "from within"). To violate—or even simply to neglect—forms "from below" (or "from without") is the very opposite of transcending them. Outwardly man must observe traditional forms as perfectly as possible. This is required for the aspirant's assimilation to the created Logos, as has been explained above. Man can only offer to God—and so transcend—what he has perfected.

Mysticism is the reality of man's love for God and man's union with God. It is a hymn to Subjectivity, a hymn to Objectivity, a hymn to Joy or Union—these three Divine Hypostases being one. It has been stressed how, contrary to certain appearances and contrary to a commonly heard opinion, mysticism is always a flowering within an orthodox framework. But, since mysticism transcends forms "from above" (or "from within"), mysticism knows no bounds. Its essence is one with the Absolute and the Infinite. Let us therefore give the last word to Jalâl ad-Dîn Rûmî, one of the greatest mystics of Islam and one of the greatest mystical poets of all time:

> I am neither Christian nor Jew nor Parsi nor Muslim. I am neither of the East nor of the West, neither of the land nor of the sea. . . . I have put aside duality and have seen that the two worlds are one. I seek the One, I know the One, I see the One, I invoke the One. He is the First, He is the Last, He is the Outward, He is the Inward.

15. THE ROLE OF OBEDIENCE IN SPIRITUALITY

Obedience is the surrendering of one's will to the will of another. It is an essential component of human life. Its origin is in man's primary vocation, which is the absolute obligation of obedience to God. Let it be said right away, that obedience is a form of death. Surrendering of the will, be it voluntary or enforced, is nothing else. But this "death" is the price of "life": "Whosoever will save his life shall lose it, and whosoever will lose his life for My sake will find it" (*Matthew*, 16, 25). This paradox inherent in life—that the price of life is death and that the price of freedom is "slavehood" to God—is the result of the Fall, or rather, of man's essential need to reverse the effects thereof. The price is high, but the reward is great. "In His will is our peace" (Dante); "Thou hast made us for Thyself, O God, and our hearts are restless till they rest in Thee" (St. Augustine); "It is in giving that we receive and it is in dying that we are born to eternal life" (St. Francis of Assisi).

Each stage in life has its specific and characteristic virtue: the virtue of childhood is, precisely, obedience. The virtue of youth is abstention and apprenticeship; the virtue of maturity is responsibility and mastership [of self, profession, of family]; and the virtue of old age is renunciation and detachment. Obedience is a reality throughout each stage of life, but our first experience of it is in childhood. Obedience is owed by the child to his parents: he must obey his parents promptly and willingly.

Chronologically and logically, following upon obedience to parents, comes obedience to the spiritual authority. This too must be wholehearted. Then comes obedience in what may be called secondary but still important spheres: to one's teacher, to one's master; on a broader canvas, to one's king or liege-lord; also to one's superior in all manner of secondary but legitimate fields: of the wife to the husband, and (having come the full circle) of children to parents.

The obligation of obedience is inescapable. Because of the Fall, our will is perverse, our ego is made of pride. Hence the need of radical and painful measures to break or rather tame it; to make it fit for salvation.

As mentioned at the outset, the essence or source of all obedience is man's primary obligation of obedience to God; all the secondary obediences, on the other hand, are to superiors, who, as the recipients of obedience, are the "representatives" of God; if they were not such, there would be no obligation to obey them. Obedience to the "representatives" of God may be described as total, but in fact only obedience to God Himself is absolute. This means that obedience to the "representatives" of God (especially the further down the line we get) is in fact less than total; it is conditional on the "rank", and on the personal worthiness, of the "representative".

By "rank" is meant the following: leaving aside all question of personal worthiness, and taking Christendom as our example, there is a greater need to obey the pope or the king than the parish priest. As for "worthiness", it is no sin to remember that, with the exception of saints, all the so-called "representatives" of God are themselves fallen men, and when their errors and shortcomings are only too visible and manifestly outweigh the privileges and prerogatives of their status, the duty of obedience to them becomes relative. Thus, even a young child owes no obedience to a perverse or abusive parent, and a wife is freed from obedience to an excessively arbitrary, selfish, or arrogant husband; many heroes have revolted against unjust kings; and many pious souls have abandoned obedience to false popes.

In the present day and age, a wife's duty of obedience to her husband may be little more than symbolic. An individual wife may be superior in virtue to her husband, or vice versa. It is a question of putting everything in its proper place, with humility, generosity, and love. Since the husband is symbolically superior, the onus is on him not to forget responsibility and sacrifice, and the fact that *noblesse oblige.*

Obedience is connected with the Fear of God. But Fear of God is but the *beginning* of wisdom (*Proverbs*, 9, 10). Integral wisdom is the Fear, Love, and Knowledge of God. We must fear God and obey Him, but we must also love Him and know Him. "Perfect love casteth out fear" (*1 John*, 4, 18). "Ye shall know the Truth, and the Truth shall make you free" (*John*, 8, 32). "Henceforth I call you not servants, for the servant knoweth not what his lord doeth; but I have called you friends, for all things that I have heard of my Father I have made known unto you" (*John*, 15, 15).

16. SPIRITUALITY IN ISLAM
Aspects of Islamic Esoterism

Islamic esoterism—or spirituality—is the inner essence of the religion of Islam. It is known as Sufism (in Arabic *tasawwuf*, from the word *suf*, "wool"), a reference to the woolen robe worn by the earliest adepts or Sufis).

In its fullness, Sufism comprises *sharî'a*, *haqîqa*, and *tarîqa*, that is to say "exoterism", "esoterism", and a spiritual or initiatic path. The relationship between the three is frequently described as follows: the *sharî'a* (the "Law" or outward form) is comparable to the circumference of a circle, the *haqîqa* (the "Total Truth" or inward essence) is comparable to the circle's center, and the radius that proceeds from circumference to center represents the spiritual or "initiatic" path (*tarîqa*), which leads from outward observance to inward conviction, from belief to vision, from potency to act. This geometrical metaphor enables us to see immediately that, since there are many radii, there are many spiritual paths. The name *tarîqa* also has the meaning of "a spiritual brotherhood".

Sufism, while outwardly conforming, is inwardly free. The *sharî'a*, the outward Law, is the doorway that opens onto inward freedom, it is the "strait path that leadeth unto life". For the Sufi, the "doorway" is not an end in itself, but it remains, at least in its essential features, a venerable and necessary framework. Christian doctrine expresses the same truth in a much more extreme manner when, in the words of St. Paul, it contrasts "the letter that killeth" with "the spirit that giveth life".

To embark on a spiritual path or *tarîqa*, a rite of initiation is necessary. Whereas in Islam, as in most religions, only some (those with a spiritual calling) receive this rite, in Christianity (which is an "esoterism" by definition) *all* adherents receive it, for baptism (which is conferred on all) is in Christianity the rite of initiation. This is a particularly striking example of what is meant by the "exoteric application" of a rite which in itself carries an esoteric grace—a grace which in fact will never be fully exploited by the vast majority of those receiving it. This is indeed "folly to the Greeks", since it is a state of affairs—a "scandal"!—virtually unheard of elsewhere.

In view of the fact that a rite of initiation is indispensable for making a beginning on the spiritual path, the latter is sometimes referred to as the "initiatic" path.

Members of a *tarîqa* are called Sufis. In principle this term should be applied only to those who have attained the goal, but in practice it is applied, not only to spiritual masters, but also to their initiated disciples. Upon initiation, an aspirant attaches himself to a *sheikh*, more or less in the same way as a Hindu devotee attaches himself to a *guru*, or as a Russian hesychast attaches himself to a *staretz*.

It has sometimes been alleged that Sufism arose from borrowings from other religions, for example Christianity, Neoplatonism, and even Hinduism and ancient Egyptian religion (from the teachings of Hermes Trismegistos—known to the ancient Egyptians as Thoth—in other words Hermeticism, a philosophy well-known to the medieval Christian schools of Western Europe). One should not, however, overestimate the role played by "borrowing", as spiritual pioneers scouting out the same territory have the same landmarks to describe, whether they use their own or someone else's terminology.

Esoterism is the correlative of exoterism. The latter is the outward and general religion of dogmas and observances to which, in a traditional society, the whole community adheres, and which promises, and provides the means of achieving, salvation. The former is the "total truth" (spiritually speaking) which lies behind—and is only symbolically expressed by—the dogmas of the general religion, and at the same time it is the key to, and the *raison d'être* of, the outward religious observances. What, in exoterism, are dogmas and observances, become, in esoterism, unconditioned or pure truth and means of spiritual realization. In both exoterism and esoterism the same two poles are present: theory and practice, or doctrine and method; they are simply envisaged at different levels. The first of these two poles, incidentally, clearly has a primary role or function: one must understand before one can do. Any practice without theory lacks both motivation and goal.

Exoterism is interested: it aims at transforming the collectivity, and saving as many souls as possible. Esoterism is disinterested and impersonal. As "total truth", it "saves" *a fortiori* but, whereas exoterism, to be itself, inevitably has a moralizing and to some extent subjectivistic character, esoterism is dispassionate and totally objective. In this connection, Frithjof Schuon writes:

> The prerogative of the human state is objectivity, the essential content of which is the Absolute. There is no *knowledge* without

Indication of the Brotherhoods (*bayân at-turuq*)
These words are inscribed on the crescent

At the foot of the trunk is the Divine Name *Allâh*. Above this are the names of Gabriel and Mohammed. The four large leaves at the top of the trunk bear the names of the first four Caliphs. The names of the brotherhoods are inscribed on the leaves.

On the five-pointed star (symbol of the Five Pillars of Islam) are the words "The Book (the Koran) and the *Sunna* (the custom of Mohammed)".

> objectivity of the intelligence, no *freedom* without objectivity of the will, and no *nobility* without objectivity of the soul. Esoterism seeks to realize pure and direct objectivity; this is its reason for being.

Seen thus, true "esoterism" is the only key to knowledge, freedom, and nobility; it is the only source of the objective and the absolute, and the only complete antidote to error. Esoterism, as understood here, is identical with traditional philosophy (for example, Platonism, Thomism, or any other venerable wisdom-system). It is not the enemy of revealed religion, as those familiar only with the many contemporary pseudo-esoterisms have found reason to suppose. Schuon continues: "Just as rationalism can remove faith, so esoterism can restore it."

Let me add that, in spite of certain differences of nuance, the terms "esoterism", "mysticism", and "spirituality" may be regarded as synonymous.

*

* *

What the Sufis were expressing, in the forms most appropriate to their perspective and their religion, was that "wisdom uncreate" (as St. Augustine called it), which is most commonly known as the *philosophia perennis*, and which reappears, in different clothing but, always essentially the same, in the Far East, among the Hindus, in ancient Ireland and Gaul, among the Sioux, and among the early Christian hermits of the Egyptian desert—that wisdom which the Bible describes in the words: "From the beginning and before the world was I created, and unto the world to come I shall not cease to be."[1] The clearest description comes from Frithjof Schuon, who writes:

> The term *philosophia perennis*, which has been current since the time of the Renaissance and of which neo-scholasticism made much use, signifies the totality of primordial and universal truths—and therefore of the metaphysical axioms—whose formulation does not belong to any particular system. One could speak in the same sense

[1] *Ecclesiasticus*, 24, 14. See also: *Ecclesiasticus*, 1, 1 and *Proverbs*, 8, 22 ff. The first and last of these passages are used in the Catholic liturgical offices of the Blessed Virgin Mary, who is herself a manifestation of the *sancta sophia* and who in her cosmic aspect has a role analogous to the "Guarded Tablet" (*al-lauh al-mahfûz*) of Islamic esoterism.

> of a *religio perennis*, designating by this term the essence of every religion; this means the essence of every form of worship, every form of prayer and every system of morality, just as the *sophia perennis* is the essence of all dogmas and all expressions of wisdom. We prefer the term *sophia* to that of *philosophia*, for the simple reason that the second term is less direct and because it evokes in addition associations of ideas with a completely profane and all too often aberrant system of thought.

The various revealed religions are sometimes represented as sectors of a circle, the sectors, by definition, coming together at the central point. The larger and wider area of each sector, bordering on the circumference, represents a given exoterism; the smaller and narrower area of the sector, which is close to the center, is the corresponding esoterism; and the dimensionless center itself is esoterism in the pure state: the total truth.

The same symbolism can also be represented in three dimensions, in the form of a cone or a mountain. Here it will be said that "all paths lead to the same summit". Once again the dimensionless central point (this time the summit of the mountain) represents the total truth. The cone or the mountain is made up of sectors, each one representing a given religion. The lower slopes of each sector represent a given exoterism, while the upper slopes of the same sector represent the corresponding esoterism. The summit represents esoterism in the pure state.

Perhaps the most direct of all the symbolisms referring to the genesis, mutual relationship, and saving role of the various revelations, is that which likens esoterism (in the pure state) to the uncolored light, and the various religions to red, green, yellow, and the other colors of the spectrum. Depending on their distance from the source of light, the colored rays will be more intense or more weak (i.e. more esoteric or more exoteric). Each color is a form or a vehicle of the truth (a refraction of the uncolored light). Each color "represents" the total truth (the uncolored light). But the supra-formal truth, the plenitude of uncolored light, is not exhausted by or limited to one single color.

Incidentally, this symbolism has the merit of showing, amongst many other things, just how precious exoterism is. A weak, colored, light shining in unfavorable circumstances is itself sufficient (if we genuinely try to see by it) to save us from outer darkness. Despite "refraction" (and let us remember that it is precisely its "color" which makes it accessible to the majority of men), and despite its apparent weakness, it is the same light as the uncolored light of God, and its merciful role is precisely to lead us back to its own absolute and infinite source.

All this has important practical consequences: one cannot take the view that, since mysticism or esoterism is the inner truth common to all the religions (namely the *religio perennis*), one can dispense with religion (exoterism) and seek only mysticism (esoterism). Man's situation is such that it is only with God's grace that he can be made worthy of turning towards the uncolored light, and he must do so by way of "red", "green", or some other color. (And his "red" or "green" must be as pure and intense as possible).

It is important to add that syncretism (or "new-ageism" of any kind) is likewise vain. To pick and choose bits and pieces from each religion (allegedly those relating to an imagined "highest common factor") is to try to mix the immiscible. Such mixing does not lead to clarity; mixing the different colors does not produce white, but rather the color of mud.

Traditional Wisdom and Modern Errors

The present age abounds in all manner of false spiritualities. The central error shared by virtually all modern cults is the fatal confusion of "spirit" and "soul". According to traditional metaphysics (ancient Greek, Medieval Scholastic, and Islamic, amongst others), man is made up of three distinct elements, namely Spirit (or Intellect), soul, and body (*See the first table on p. 46.*)

The "Spirit" (or "Intellect"), although "created", is supra-formal or universal, and directly touched by the Divine. It is the only supra-individual, "archetypal", and *objective* element in man's constitution. Spirit and Intellect are the two sides of the same coin, the latter pertaining to Truth (or doctrine) and the former to Being (or realization). The soul, on the other hand, is formal and individual. The Spirit is therefore the "measure" of the soul; the soul can never be the "measure" of the Spirit.[2] The error of a psychologist such as Jung lies in the complete confusion of Spirit and soul, which in practice amounts to an "abolition" of Spirit. The consequence of this is the "abolition" of the absolute and the blocking of access to the all-important element

[2] Amongst the soul's faculties are: mind (or reason), will, affect (or sentiment), imagination, and memory. (*See the second table on p. 46*). In modern parlance, "intellect" is often misleadingly used to signify mind or reason, whereas, traditionally, it is synonymous with "Spirit". There is no impenetrable barrier between mind (or reason) and Intellect: the relationship of the latter to the former is like the relationship of the pinnacle of a cone to its circumferential base.

of objectivity. We are left stranded in a satanic kingdom where everything (truth, morality, art) is relative! Only the ancient world religions, in their traditional form, can oppose the new-age of cults.

It is precisely because of the anti-Platonic, anti-Aristotelian, and anti-Thomistic character of the modern age (epitomized by the nefarious Teilhard de Chardin), that one can say that its chief intellectual characteristic is the "abolition" of the absolute and of objectivity. Quite simply, it is an age of "nominalism", existentialism, and error, in which relativism and subjectivism run riot, with catastrophic results for both the individual and society. The only antidote to the relative and the subjective is the absolute and the objective, and it is precisely they that are the contents of traditional metaphysics or the *philosophia perennis.*

Islam in the Modern World

In closing, a final observation—strictly speaking outside our present subject, but not entirely without relevance—should perhaps be made: the first prerequisite for understanding the religion of Islam is to disengage it entirely in our minds from current news reports emerging from Islamic countries, and also from the hostile opinions and attitudes which these reports arouse in the West. The pronouncements occasionally made by the highly dubious leaders of many of the Islamic countries serve only to reinforce the negative reactions. It is true that, in the 20th century, there were—and there may still be—a good number of honorable Islamic countries and Islamic rulers,[3] but the countries and the rulers that are now mostly in the news are usually anything but truly Islamic. Some of the rulers are modern revolutionaries clothing themselves in "literalism" and "fundamentalism"; some are frank secularists (who, in spite of their secularism, sometimes turn to using religion for political ends). Modern politics has cast a blight on many (indeed almost all) sectors of the world, not merely the Islamic. Sometimes, of course, bad press and television reports from Islamic countries are untrue and unfair, and one has to look at least a little beneath the surface to uncover the true situation.[4]

[3] One thinks, for example, of distinguished leaders such as Abu Bakar Tafawa Balewa of Nigeria, Tungku Abd ar-Rahman of Malaysia, and King Idris of Libya.

[4] Very different from today's antagonism was the relationship between Christians and Muslims during the many centuries of Moorish rule in Spain. At that time, both religions were still robust and authentic, and not yet denatured. For enlightening details regarding this communal symbiosis, see *Spain under the Crescent Moon* by Angus Macnab (Fons Vitae, Louisville KY, 1999).

17. SPIRITUALITY IN CHRISTIANITY
A Visit to Mount Athos

A journey to Mount Athos (the Eastern Orthodox monastic community situated on a peninsula in the north-eastern corner of Greece) is much more than a merely physical journey. It is inevitably something of a pilgrimage, since it involves leaving a world of forgetfulness and entering a world of remembrance: remembrance of God is the reason for being of the Holy Mountain (*Hagion Oros*).

The evangelical doctrine that contemplation is superior to action (or, in an even more precise terminology, that contemplation is the highest form of *action*) finds expression, down to the present day, in the life of Mount Athos. Not only is the monks' work (which is usually extremely hard physically) subordinated to their spiritual life, it is also made to serve as an outward support for the latter.

On the Mount Athos peninsula one finds examples of every type of Eastern Orthodox contemplative life: there are "cenobitic" monasteries, "idiorrhythmic" monasteries, "sketes", and hermitages. During a visit to Mount Athos in 1954, a Swiss friend and myself had the privilege of spending a few days in close contact with each of these modes of monastic life and, now more than fifty years later, it may be of interest to recall some of the details of this unique journey.

In the cenobitic monasteries, all activities come under the central direction of the Abbot, and attendance at the monastery church for Divine Office is compulsory. Amongst the monasteries of this kind which we visited were St. Paul, St. Simon Peter, and St. Pandeleimon, the first two being Greek and the third Russian. In these monasteries we frequently attended Divine Office with the monks. At mealtimes we would sit in the refectory in silence, eating vegetables, fruit, and sometimes fish, while a monk would read aloud from the Gospels or the lives of the saints. No meat is eaten on Mount Athos, and when the monks are fasting (which is frequently) they also abstain from fish. It will be seen, therefore, that all that remains for their sustenance is bread, vegetables, fruit, and wine (*retsina*). Since the ban on female creatures' setting foot on the peninsula extends even to hens and cows, there are neither eggs nor cheese, though it is permitted to import such things from Greece.

The idiorrhythmic monasteries which we visited included Iviron and Xiropotamou. Here a certain amount of individual initiative is permitted with regard to the communal recitation of the Office. In these monasteries the monks are also entitled to have certain personal belongings. The greater freedom from routine permits visitors more opportunity for personal contacts and private conversation, although in fact we found that this was also perfectly possible in the cenobitic monasteries. In both types of monastery the work of self-maintenance involved fairly hard physical labor: collecting provisions, gathering wood, making long trips on foot over rough stony pathways to the local jetty or "port", doing repairs, etc. The monks usually attend to the various duties in turn, but in the richer monasteries they may also employ lay Greek tradesmen and laborers to assist them.

In all the monasteries we visited, we enjoyed numerous exchanges with the monks, especially during the long evenings, when we would sit with our hosts on a monastery balcony, sipping Turkish coffee and admiring the beauty of the calm sea and the magnificent sunset. Since neither of us knew Greek, these (for us) valuable conversations had to be conducted in one or other of those Western European languages of which we had some knowledge, and consequently we always had to seek out monks who had some familiarity with English, French, or German.

The "sketes" are small cottages where "two or three are gathered together" to lead a life of prayer or "remembrance of God". Usually two or three monks of different ages share a small house, with its own altar or "church", the older monks instructing the younger ones in the ways of work and prayer. The sketes are usually to be found in small groups or villages, each of which has a central church (in addition to the small churches or oratories to be found in the houses themselves). There is a beautiful collection of sketes at St. Anne's (Hagia Anna) on the southern side of the peninsula between Daphne and Karoulia. Here we stayed for three days with two charming hosts (Brother Artemis and Brother Ilias) who showed us in detail the ways of their daily life, the working part of which consisted of spinning and weaving with goat hair, and making many different articles therefrom. All such activities are performed within the framework of the Divine Office, the constant recitation of which imposes a supernatural rhythm and pattern on the monks' lives.

The monks (who are not priests) recite the Office on their own, while the liturgy is celebrated and the sacraments administered by the priest in the central church.

St. Simon Peter's Monastery, Mount Athos

On the extreme tip of the Athos peninsula, in the district known as Karoulia, we were able to spend two nights with a hermit in his hut. The hermit was an aged Russian peasant called Brother Zóssima, and his life, as might be expected, was one of considerable austerity. Nevertheless here too the spiritual predominated over the physical, not only in the form of the hermit's frequent—indeed continual—prayer, but also by his regular visits, involving quite hazardous cliff-edge journeys, to the nearest church to attend the liturgy and receive the sacraments.

In this part of Athos we met several hermits living in a state of isolation, not only from the "world", but also from the monasteries and sketes in the more accessible parts of the peninsula. Most notable amongst these was Father Nicone, a priest and monk whom (thanks to an introduction from Mr. Gerald Palmer, who was his disciple) I had met in 1950 in Geneva and Lausanne during his one and only visit outside Athos since taking up residence there. Father Nicone was a Russian aristocrat who had been an officer in the Tsarist army and was a personal friend of several of the existing crowned heads of Europe. He spoke all Western European languages with wit and to perfection. In Lausanne I had had the good fortune to spend much time with him (both in the company of others and alone), and when I visited him on Mount Athos, he had the humility and generosity to receive me as an old friend. On my departure from Athos a few days later, he had occasion to be in the port of Daphne, and he saw me off on the small boat. In 1950, amongst many other things, he had told me: "Orthodoxy is purity." Now he said: "Henceforth, wherever you go, you must always carry the Holy Mountain (*Hagion Oros*) with you in your heart."

One must not fail to make mention of the beautiful land of Athos itself. It is dedicated to the Virgin Mary and is called the "garden of Our Lady"; indeed it vividly evokes the virginal qualities of purity, mercy, and beauty. Through the presence of the Virgin—and in spite of the physical absence of female creatures—an atmosphere of celestial femininity seems to permeate both life and landscape.

The natural symbols of the different aspects of the spiritual life are strikingly represented: the high mountain; the flash of lightning; the calm sea; the luxuriant vegetation; the pale moon; the brilliant sun. In the midst of these visible reminders of the invisible Creator, steeped in the Gospels and the patristic writings, and far from the world of evolutionism, progressivism, scientism, and psychologism, the monks find an ambience of beauty that is evocative of Truth and conducive to its contemplation.

Everywhere we went we observed the monks' profound attachment to their way of life and their capacity to explain it; we listened to many reasoned expositions of Eastern monasticism. At one monastery we were shown the original statutes or charters granted to Mount Athos by the Turkish sultans. These manuscript documents were in a beautiful Arabic script, and invariably began with the Arabic words: "In the Name of God, the Clement, the Merciful." They guaranteed the monks' religious freedom, and also the independence of the monastic government. Some of the monks told us that the community had fared better under the Muslim Turks than under the secularism of modern Greek nationalism.

The operative or methodic side of Athonite spirituality is the "prayer of Jesus". This is the constant repetition—in obedience to St. Paul's injunction to "pray without ceasing" (*1 Thessalonians*, 5, 17)—of a formula based on the words of the publican in Christ's parable (*Luke*, 18, 9-14) who, unlike the Pharisee, "would not lift up so much his eyes unto Heaven, but smote upon his breast, saying: 'God be merciful to me a sinner'". To these words, the Church added the name of Christ, so that the full formula became: "Lord Jesus Christ, Son of God, be merciful to me a sinner" (in Greek: *Kýrie 'Iêsoé Christé hyié Theoû 'eleisòn me hamartolòn*). This formula appears in the Roman liturgy in the words (conserved in the original Greek) *Kýrie 'eleisòn, Christé 'eleisòn.* The Jesus prayer has been made familiar in the West in the story of the "Russian Pilgrim",[1] and not a few of our encounters on the Holy Mountain brought the pages of this little book vividly to mind.

The theological basis of this current of Christian spirituality is to be found in the writings of St. Gregory Palamas, "whose doctrine", as Frithjof Schuon has observed, "is of fundamental importance for Orthodox theology and represents a strictly traditional synthesis of the teachings of the Fathers such as St. Dionysius the Areopagite and St. Gregory of Nyssa, and indeed of all the Greek Fathers right back to the Apostles".[2]

The essence of St. Gregory's teaching (which has come to be known as "Palamitism") is none other than the doctrine of deification, which finds its most concise expression in the formula, first used by St. Irenaeus: "God became man ['Incarnation'] so that man might become God ['Deification']." (*Autós gar 'enanthrôpêsen* [*'Sarkosis'*]

[1] See *The Way of a Pilgrim.*

[2] *The Transcendent Unity of the Religions* (1st edition, Faber, London, 1953), p. 176.

hina hêmeîs theopöiëthômen [*'Theôsis'*]). This formulation is also found in the writings of St. Athanasius, St. Gregory of Nazianzus, and St. Gregory of Nyssa, and is repeated by the Greek Fathers throughout the centuries.

The teachings of these Fathers and of the Eastern Church in general have been lucidly expounded in the writings of Vladimir Lossky.[3] Perhaps the most "essential" exposition of Orthodox mystical theology is to be found in *La doctrine de la "déification" dans l'Église grecque jusqu'au XIe siècle* by M. Lot-Borodine.[4] An acquaintance with these doctrines is a great advantage for the visitor or student of Mount Athos, since it is from them that are derived the various spiritual practices that have come to be regarded as characteristically Athonite.

The most important source book in this connection is the collection of writings of the Greek Fathers known as the *Philokalia*, part of which has appeared in an excellent English translation.[5]

The spiritual method which finds its embodiment on Mount Athos and which derives from the doctrine of deification is known as "hesychasm" (from the Greek *hesychía*, "quiet"). Hesychasm amounts to a whole-hearted commitment to the practice of the Jesus prayer. Over and above the retention of the words *Christé 'eleisôn* in the Catholic liturgy, the methodic invocation of the Holy Name appears in the West encrusted in the Dominican rosary, the full recitation of which involves the enunciation of the name of Jesus one hundred and fifty-three times. Several great Medieval saints, such as St. Bernard of Clairvaux and St. Francis of Assisi, practiced the systematic invocation of the Holy Name, and a renowned 16th century practitioner and teacher of this method was St. Bernardino of Siena. The practice has been revived in modern times by the writings of the Italian nun Sister Consolata.[6] For recent Orthodox presentations of the theory and prac-

[3] See especially *The Mystical Theology of the Eastern Church* (Clarke, London, 1957).

[4] Published in *La revue de l'histoire des religions*, 1947.

[5] See *Writings from the Philokalia* (with an anonymous Foreword by the late Father Nicone, priest and hermit on Mount Athos, who also selected the material to be translated) (Faber, London, 1951), and *Early Fathers from the Philokalia* (Faber, London, 1954), both volumes translated by Mrs. E. Kadloubovsky and Mr. Gerald Palmer.

[6] See *Jesus Appeals to the World*.

tice of the prayer of Jesus, see André Bloom (Archbishop Anthony),[7] Maurice Aniane,[8] and Timothy Ware (Bishop Kallistos).[9]

Philip Sherrard's two books *Athos, the Mountain of Silence*[10] and *Athos, the Holy Mountain*[11] are valuable historical and theological surveys of the spirituality of Mount Athos and both are beautifully illustrated.

*

* *

The beauty and grandeur of Mount Athos cannot fail to elicit respect and love. A visit is precious because it allows a personal contact with the monks and their way of life, and also with the beautiful natural ambience of orchards, stony pathways, cliffs, and sea. Far away from Mount Athos, one can be permanently near in spirit by being mindful of the principles which inspire its life and worship.[12]

[7] In *Yoga, science de l'homme intégral* (*Cahiers du Sud*, Paris, 1953).

[8] *Ibid.*, p. 243.

[9] *The Power of the Name: The Jesus Prayer in Orthodox Spirituality* (Sisters of the Love of God Press, Convent of the Incarnation, Fairacres, Oxford, 1974).

[10] Oxford University Press, 1960.

[11] The Alexandria Press (London) and the Overlook Press (Woodstock, N.Y)., 1982.

[12] It is not my purpose in this chapter to discuss the schism between the Eastern and Western Churches or the contentious doctrine of the *Filioque* which was its cause. See p. 25, fn.1 and the Glossary (p. 142).

18. SPIRITUALITY IN HINDUISM
A Visit to the Jagadguru

Historically speaking, there can be little doubt that the greatest exponent ever of pure and unconditional metaphysics made his appearance in the world of Hinduism. This was Shankara, who lived in India in the 9th century A.D. He is often referred to as Shrî Shankarâchârya. In India, *Shrî*, the literal Sanskrit meaning of which is "Lord", is widely used as an honorific, and *achârya* means "teacher". The metaphysical doctrine of Shankara is known as *advaita* or "non-dualism"—a double negative, so to speak, which has its parallels in the Neoplatonic expression "the One without a second" and in the Islamic expression "He who has no associate" (*lâ sharîka la-Hu*).

Shankara's function was to formulate the truth, to give expression to ultimate reality. There is an authentic line of spiritual descent from the original Shankarâchârya down to the present day. It is refracted into five traditional functions or offices, all of them regular and valid. All five of the holders of these offices bear the title of *Shankarâchârya*, and these Shankarâchâryas have their official seats respectively at Badrinath (in the north), Puri (in the east), Dwarkâ (in the west), Kanchipuram (in the south), and Sringeri (also in the south). Each Shankarâchârya also has the title of *Jagadguru* or "universal teacher" (*jagad* literally signifying "world").

There are many paths that lead to God. In India, as elsewhere, the one that is most widespread is that of "devotion" (*bhakti*). However, for their respective regions of India, these spiritual descendents of the original Shankarâchârya traditionally and symbolically represent the uncolored light of knowledge or gnosis (*jñâna*).

During a visit to India in March-April of 1963, I accompanied two of his Indian devotees on a visit to the Shankarâchârya of Kanchipuram. Kanchipuram (in Sanskrit, "Golden City") is in Madras State (*Tamilnad*), and in the Tamil language it is known as Conjeeveram.

Each Shankarâchârya has, so to speak, a circuit: that is to say, he travels publicly and ceremonially, accompanied by his suite. In the case of the Jagadguru of Kanchipuram, the suite includes elephants, camels, cows, and musicians. For the collectivity in general, he exercises his function in a manner that the Buddhists might describe as an "activity of presence": he is a blessing, not merely for what he teaches, but above all for what he (or his office) *is*. In this respect at least, his

The 68th Shankarâchârya (the Jagadguru) of Kanchipuram (1894-1994)

role is analogous to, and has the importance of, that of a temporal monarch. (Miraculously, this role still has validity even in modern and democratic monarchies which have long since forgotten their traditional and sacred past.)

At the moment concerned, the Jagadguru was known to be at Tanjore, and we set forth from Madras on the afternoon of 3 April 1963. The journey was of approximately two hundred miles, and it took about seven or eight hours to complete it. On the way we passed through the towns of Pondicherry, Cuddalore, Chidambaram, and Kumbakonam, and arrived at Tanjore fairly late at night. It was a beautiful drive, both during the daylight hours and after dark, when we traversed the Tamilnad countryside by full moon. (I had already visited the towns of Chidambaram and Tanjore on my way from the southern tip of India to Madras.)

In Pondicherry, we stopped for a moment at the "ashram" of the late Aurobindo, the modernist-evolutionist pseudo-mystic, where one of our party had some minor errand to perform. I did not get out of the car. A few signs of the erstwhile French presence in Pondicherry were still visible, such as the imposing Catholic church "Notre Dame des Anges", a statue of St. Joan of Arc, and, less sublimely, the name of the main square: Place Charles de Gaulle! In the delightful small town of Kumbakonam, we stopped for a while, and took photographs of the magnificent temple with its large square enclosure, impressive towers (*gopurams*), and "tank" (*teppakulam*). Here we seemed to be at the very heart of Hindu India. On reaching Tanjore, we took a room at the Rajah Guest House.

Next morning, having risen early, we went out to purchase some fruit which we could later offer to the Jagadguru. After seeking vainly for a long time, we finally obtained this from a Muslim fruit-seller named 'Abd al-Quddûs ("the slave of the All-Holy"), who had a shop near the railway station. Then we made our way to the place where the Jagadguru and his entourage were camped—a spot just south-west of the Brihadeshwara Temple.

The Jagadguru's full designation is: His Holiness the Jagadguru Shrî Chandrasekharendra Sarasvati, the 68th Shankarâchârya Svâmigal of Kânchî Kâmakoti Pîtha. He was born in 1894, and assumed his function in 1907. He died in 1994 at the age of 99 years. His successor, Shrî Jayendra Sarasvati, had been appointed many years before his death, and it is now he who, as the 69th Shankarâchârya Svâmigal, fills the role of head of the Kâmakoti Math (Mathâdhipati). A successor to the last-named, known as the junior Svâmigal, was also appointed during the life-time of the 68th Shankarâchârya, and thus at the time of my visit in 1963, three "generations" of Shankarâchâryas were present in Kanchi.

On the occasion of his death, an appreciation of the 68th Shankarâchârya was published in *Time Magazine* (24 January 1994). Mention was made of his friendship with Mahatma Gandhi, and of his deep knowledge of Christianity. Like another great Hindu spiritual figure of the 20th century, Swami Ramdas, he also had a profound respect for Islam, and the Indian Prime Minister mourned him as "one who symbolized peace and harmony in a turbulent world".

Preliminary arrangements for an audience had previously been made, and we now informed members of the Jagadguru's entourage of our arrival. Usually, at this stage, a period of waiting is involved, sometimes extending to several days. Devotees regard the waiting-period as a sort of "retreat" and give it over to spiritual preparation and prayer.

To our great surprise, however, as soon as the Jagadguru had been informed of our arrival, he let it be known that he would receive us at once. My companions hastened to prepare themselves in matters of dress. The proper dress is a *dhoti*, with bare chest and bare feet. The two devotees were dressed thus and, as Vaishnava *brahmins*, also applied the mark of Vishnu to their foreheads. (The Jagadguru, descendent of the original Shankarâchârya, is a Shaiva.) I was wearing European dress, but I removed my shirt, shoes and socks, and thus appeared, suitably bare-chested, to merge acceptably with my two companions. Our preparations took less than five minutes.

On entering the compound, we found the Jagadguru sitting cross-legged on a mat, and with a staff in his hand, just as he most often appears in photographs. We prostrated ourselves before him in the prescribed manner. We offered him the fruit that we had brought with us, and he motioned us to sit down on a mat near him. The only others present in the compound were his *aide-de-camp* and a servant.

All remained silent for some moments. Then His Holiness put some questions regarding the European visitor: where he came from, what his profession was, etc. The Jagadguru spoke mainly in Kanarese, the language of Mysore, from which the Jagadguru—and did also, as it happened, the two devotees—originated. The two friends kindly interpreted for my benefit. The Jagadguru also spoke a little in Tamil, and occasionally used English expressions. He knows English well, but normally does not speak it.

The Jagadguru then referred to Frithjof Schuon, concerning whom he was well aware, since the latter had dedicated his book *Language of the Self* to him. This had been mediated by Mr. Macleod Matheson, one of the translators of the book, who visited the Jagadguru in February 1959, presented him with the English manuscript, and received the Jagadguru's acceptance of the dedication. The book was published in India later that year. His Holiness referred to the chapter in the book dealing with the sacred pipe of the North American Indians, and also to the book *Black Elk Speaks*, and said that the rites of the Red Man resembled those of Hinduism. He then spoke of the Algerian Sheikh Ahmad al-'Alâwî and of Martin Lings' impressive monograph on him, *A Sufi Saint of the Twentieth Century*, which had been published in 1961.

Having mentioned the Jagadguru's interest in Schuon's book, and in the rites of the Plains Indians, it is appropriate to recall that Schuon, in his book *The Feathered Sun*, refers to a meeting that he had, during his first visit to North America in 1959, with a holy man of the Cheyenne tribe. Schuon showed the venerable elder a picture of the Jagadguru, and spoke to him of the spirituality of Hinduism. The Cheyenne priest took the picture in one hand, and raised the other towards the sky—the Red Indian gesture of prayer. He prayed a long time while gazing at the picture, and finally put his hand on it and then, in the Red Indian manner, rubbed his face and breast with his hand so as to impregnate himself with the Jagadguru's blessing. Finally, he reverently kissed the picture.

Our discussion with the Jagadguru then turned to the dissemination in Europe and North America, thanks to the Guénon-Schuon books, of the ideas of metaphysics, intellectuality, orthodoxy, and tradition. Reference was made to the three forms of Christianity: Eastern Orthodoxy, Roman Catholicism, and Protestantism, and to the possibilities within them, in 20th century conditions, for following a spiritual path based on faith and prayer. His Holiness expressed interest in both the collective and individual prayer of these denominations, and enquired in detail about the Christian sacraments. He classified the Hindu rites as *diksha*s and *samskara*s, and made it clear from what he said that the former correspond to the sacraments of Baptism and Confirmation (which have an initiatic character), while the latter correspond to the sacraments of Eucharist, Penance, and Extreme Unction (which mediate sanctifying grace), and of Matrimony and Ordination (which confer a grace of state).

Towards the end of the audience the Jagadguru blessed the basket of fruit which we had given him, and from it gave each of us a piece of fruit, to eat later. He also blessed a photograph of himself, and presented it to me. His Holiness then gave us his blessing, which indicated that the audience was at an end. We made our obeisances, and took our leave, never turning our backs on him as we departed the compound. The whole audience lasted the best part of an hour. We returned to our guesthouse, where we ate the fruit that we had been given.

For a little while, we drove around Tanjore, and I saw again some of the sights that I had seen six days previously while on my way, by train, bus, and bullock-cart, from the southern tip of India to Madras. Soon we started on our return journey, and drove to Tiruvannamalai, where we spent the night in the ashram of the late Shrî Râmana Mahârshi, the great *jñânin* who had died in 1950. We had our evening meal (South Indian vegetarian style) in the ashram, and briefly met Mrs. MacIver, a Parsi lady, who was the widow of an early English acquaintance of René Guénon. We also met a *sadhu* ("devotee") from the ashram, at Kahangad near Mangalore, of Swami Ramdas, the great votary of the Name of *Ram*.

In the ashram of Shrî Râmana Mahârshi, we continued to visit some of the places that had been hallowed by his presence, and then went out for a delightful evening stroll. The next morning, we climbed half-way up the sacred hill of Arunachala, where we visited the samadhi (place of meditation) of the Mahârshi. From the hillside we had a splendid overview of the large temple of Tiruvannamalai and, on descending again into the village, paid a visit to it. We gave the priest in the temple a small stipend, and he offered worship on our behalf. After that, we continued on our journey, passing through the small Tamil town of Madhurantakam where, in 1884, an Englishman named Lionel Place had a vision of Shrî Rama (the seventh incarnation of Vishnu). We arrived back in Madras later in the day.

19. SPIRITUALITY IN BUDDHISM
The Meaning of Tantra

In Buddhism, there are not only the two great schools, *Hînayâna* and *Mahâyâna.* There is also a "Third School"—or a "Third Setting in Motion of the Wheel of the Law" (*Dharma-Chakra-Pravatana*)—namely a branch of *Mahâyâna* Buddhism known as *Vajrayâna* or *Tantrayâna. Vajrayâna* spread from India to Tibet in the 11th century, and became of particular importance in the latter country.

Buddhism in general looks on the world as an exile; it sees it under its negative aspect of corruptibility and temptation—and so of suffering. *Tantra*, on the contrary, sees the world positively as theophany or symbol; it sees through the forms to the essences. Its spiritual way is union with the celestial archetypes of created things. In the words of Frithjof Schuon: "*Tantra* is the spiritualization—or interiorization—of beauty, and also of natural pleasures, by virtue of the metaphysical transparency of phenomena. In a word: *Tantra* is nobility of sentiments and experiences; it excludes all excess and goes hand in hand with sobriety; it is a sense of archetypes, a return to essences and primordiality."

The metaphysical doctrine and spiritual practice of *tantra* is based on the masculine and feminine principles or "poles", known in *Vedânta* as *Purusha* and *Prakriti.* In Hinduism, these are represented or symbolized by Shiva and his Consort (*Shakti*) Kali. In *Mahâyâna* Buddhism in general, and in Tibetan Buddhism in particular, the masculine and feminine principles appear in the form of the following pairs:

Masculine		**Feminine**
Upâya ("formal doctrine and method")	—	*Prajnâ* ("formless wisdom")
Vajra ("Lightning", "Diamond")	—	*Garbha* ("Womb")
Dorje ("Thunderbolt Scepter)	—	*Dilbu* ("Handbell")
Mani ("Jewel")	—	*Padma* ("Lotus")

This polarity (and its resolution) evokes the doctrine implicit in one of the Hindu names for God, namely *Sat-Chit-Ânanda*, commonly translated as "Being-Consciousness-Bliss". *In divinis* this ternary means "Object-Subject-Union" and, spiritually or operatively, it can be rendered as "Beloved-Lover-Love" and other analogous ternaries:

Sat	Being	Object	Beloved	Invoked	Known
Chit	Consciousness	Subject	Lover	Invoker	Knower
Ânanda	Bliss	Union	Love	Invocation	Knowledge

In this context, the first row is seen as the "feminine" element (*prajnâ*), the second row as the "masculine" element (*upâya*), and the third row as the union between them (*sukha*).

Metaphysically, it can be said that *samsâra* (the world) **is** *Nirvâna* (the Divine State). This is because Reality is one, and the Principle of *samsâra* is *Nirvâna*. Also, and for the same reason, the distinction can be bridged in unitive prayer: "The Kingdom of Heaven is within you." For fallen man, however, the situation is quite different: *samsâra* is very far from *Nirvâna*. Hence the Buddha's central message: "I teach two things, O disciples, suffering and release from suffering." In theistic terms, one can say that ex-sistence, by definition, involves separation from the Divine Source. God created the world so that "other-than-God" could know Him. The purpose of existence is precisely the work of return; were it not so, existence would have no meaning. This work is compounded of faith and prayer, and rendered possible by the saving grace of the *Avatâra*. In *Vajrayâna* Buddhism, *tantra* is the Way of Return.

The operative side of tantric doctrine resides essentially in the invocatory spiritual method (*mantrayâna*), namely *Buddhânusmriti* ("remembrance of the Buddha"). In Christianity, the analogous method finds its scriptural basis in the text "Whoever shall call upon the Name of the Lord shall be saved" (*Romans*, 10, 13). This practice takes the form of the constant or frequent invocation of a sacred formula or *mantra*, the sacramental power of which derives from the Name (or Names) of the Divinity which it contains. If meditation is the emptying of the mind of worldly things, invocation is the filling of the mind (and heart) with a revealed Divine Name and its saving grace.

The masculine and feminine principles of *tantra* are present in the Names contained in the *Mani-Mantra*, the central invocatory prayer of Tibetan Buddhism, namely, *Om Mani Padme Hum*: "O Thou Jewel in the Lotus, hail!" The Jewel may be interpreted as Avalokiteshvara (the Bodhisattva representing the Buddha's Mercy or Compassion) and the Lotus as his feminine counterpart Târâ. The Lotus (*padma*) is the existential or "horizontal" support for the "vertical" or "axial" Jewel (*mani*).

The Lotus is thus the symbol of the pure and humble human soul (viewed as feminine and "horizontal") that opens out its petals (i.e. acquires the fundamental spiritual virtues) so that it may attract, and become the fitting vehicle of, the Jewel of Buddheic grace (viewed as masculine and "vertical"). This symbolism is identical to that of weaving, in which the weft (horizontal) and the warp (vertical) are in the same "sexual" relationship to one another. "Weaving" is in fact the literal meaning of the word *tantra.*

There is an obvious analogy between the Tibetan formula and similar invocatory prayers in other religions, such as *Sîtâ-Râm* in Hinduism and *Jesu-Maria* in Catholicism.

As indicated in the foregoing table, the union of the "Subject" with the "Object", of the Invoker with the Invoked, of the Lover (masculine) and with the Beloved (feminine) results in *Ânanda* or "Bliss". In Buddhist *tantra* this spiritual union is called *Mahâsukha* ("the Great Bliss"). This is symbolized in Tibetan art by the tantric statue of *Yab-Yum* (literally "father-mother"), which portrays the loving union of the masculine and the feminine principles.

ཨོཾ མ ཎི པ དྨེ ཧཱུྃ

The *mantra* Om Mani Padme Hum
("O Thou Jewel in the Lotus, hail!")

APPENDIX I
Excerpts from Letters

Editors' Note: Before finalizing our selection of excerpts from William Stoddart's letters, we contacted the author himself, who asked us to say the following: "There is much precise and incisive spiritual advice offered to my correspondents in these letters, and it is therefore essential to make it absolutely clear that this does not originate from myself, but represents no more than my best effort, at the time of writing a given letter to a given recipient, to reproduce and convey the relevant spiritual teaching of Frithjof Schuon."

General

One can read "round and about" traditional and semi-traditional matters for a very long time. The key question is whether or not one already has, or has acquired, an adequate intuition of what is essential—that is to say: truth, and conformity to truth.

Conformity to truth means: prayer, virtue, and beauty. One can therefore summarize the essential as: prayer, on the basis of truth, in a climate of virtue, and within a framework of beauty. God Himself is Truth; prayer means *remembrance* of God; virtue means humility and generosity; and beauty refers to both virgin nature and sacred art.

Of course, I agree strongly that, in a world of error, reading (i.e., reading books which expound the truth) is of prime importance. But people are unwilling to read, and they call "difficult" the only books that are worth reading.

*

* *

One can explain things only to those who wish to know—only to those who have an insatiable appetite for truth. One can teach nothing to those who "know already"—that is to say, to those who, for one reason or another, have jumped to hasty conclusions, on the basis of inadequate data. To have an appetite for truth, or to wish to be filled with truth alone, is perhaps the profoundest meaning of the Sufi expression *faqr* ("poverty" or emptiness for God). The two pillars of the spiritual way are indeed, in Sufi terms, *dhikr* and *faqr*: namely, the remembrance of God and the forgetting of self.

Without always realizing what is happening, we sometimes passively allow our views to be fashioned by those whom we choose to listen to. What Hindus call "lower *mâyâ*" (or what Christians call the seductive envy of the "world") delights in throwing the wrong informants in our path—and can make them seem like qualified informants! We must be *active*, and not *passive*, in the exercise of our discrimination. This is the very first of our God-given responsibilities. We must be *implacable* in our determination to reach the whole truth, and nothing but the truth.

We must be *fortes in fide*—strong in faith, and strong in truth. As it is said in the Book of Esdras: *Magna est veritas, et praevalebit*—Truth is great, and it shall prevail.

*

* *

Spiritual courtesy (what the Arabs call *adab*) is an integral part of the spiritual life, and consequently its fundamental principle is the same as that of spirituality in general, namely a love of truth, an engagement to conform to it, and a respect for others.

Adab inevitably involves a degree of self-sacrifice. A person does not enter a spiritual path to obtain justice, but to forget himself and to remember God. Frithjof Schuon defined pride not only as "over-estimating oneself" but also as "under-estimating others". Man is made in the image of God but, from another point of view, he is nothing, and one follows a spiritual way to realize this.

Patience, which is close to humility and self-sacrifice, is an essential key.

The twin virtues are indeed: patience and trust, gratitude and generosity, forgetting ourselves and remembering God.

We live in an age when one has to state the obvious! "2 + 2 = 4" and "a 'philosopher' means 'a lover of wisdom'"! In this sense, Descartes and Kant were certainly not philosophers! Of course it is true that, in the sense of a literary *genre*, they were "philosophers". Also, if "philosopher" simply means "one who thinks" (as, in common parlance, it does), then even Descartes and Kant were philosophers; however, since they *thought badly*, they were bad philosophers, or rather "misosophers" (haters of truth)! Only Pythagoras, Plato, Aristotle, Plotinus—and their pupils and descendants—are philosophers in the true sense of the word. And to them, of course, one must add the great Scholastics.

The Scholastics and the Greeks were "rationalists" in the sense that they used reason and logic. But they "reasoned" on the basis of true premises; on the basis of true axioms; on the basis of "revelation" and/or "intellection".

The error of Descartes, Kant, and those who followed, is that they discounted "intellectual intuition" and reasoned on the basis of bankrupt premises. Modern scientists reason on the basis of empirical data. Their fault or defect is not in their reasoning capacity, but in their lack of intuition of the higher levels of reality; in a word, in their obliviousness of the Intellect and of the Absolute. Modern scientists recognize only the material, and the lower psychic, realms. The results have been catastrophic.

*

* *

God does not owe us an easy passage. None of the Prophets had an easy passage. How can we expect better? In fact, God makes the way easier for us than he did for the Prophets. Each one of the Prophets knew, concretely and existentially, the pains and trials which face man. Life is a struggle until the moment of our death—but God's help and protection never diminish! There are many false signs; Truth—and Intelligence—are the key: they bring saving grace.

Comments on the Catholicism of the Post-Vatican II Period

The fidelity of traditional Catholics to the traditional catechism and sacraments is much to be admired; their main fault, unfortunately, is their tendency to exclusivism. It could be said that "exclusivism" is natural to human groups and is a traditional means of self-preservation. This may be true, but it leaves out of account the unprecedented nature of our present predicament, in which all religions are being eroded by the same destructive forces. Whether we are aware of it or not, the "enemy" has changed: he is no longer to be found in the "competing" religions or denominations, but in the opponents, gross and subtle, of all religion. This is not merely the affair of "esoterism"; it is a fact of experience that many sensitive "exoterists" have an effective intuition of the new situation. Such people deserve our support; they should not be undermined.

*

* *

It is the Holy Spirit, and not the Catholic Church (an *upâya*, or "saving form", in Buddhist terms), which, in the last analysis, all Catholics must obey. Obedience to the Church is purely symbolic. It is a symbol of obedience to the Holy Spirit. In these latter days, it can be dangerous to take obedience to the Church too literally (this also applies to the normal Church of pre-Vatican II). This is precisely how most Catholics were induced to accept such radical changes. They were told to "be docile". Literal obedience to the *symbol* of the Holy Spirit can actually become a *sin* against the Holy Spirit—because in extreme cases it can become superstition and idolatry. At the philosophical level, the Sufi saint and philosopher Ibn 'Arabî expressed this negative possibility with the utmost clarity; at the practical level, it has in our day been the cause of problems and divisions in Catholic communities everywhere. Troubled contemporary Catholicism suffers more from this particular error than from any other single cause.[1] This is why inward, invisible, and unswerving obedience to the *Total* Truth is the most charitable thing we can possibly perform at the present time both for ourselves and for the world at large. It is "exoterists" who are the beneficiaries of our espousal of the "total truth", even though we cannot always explicitly articulate it to them. Our inspired *silences* are eloquent, and our prayers are a blessing *pro multis*.

*

* *

Whatever else Protestantism is, it is not modern! Luther loved St. Paul and St. Augustine and hated the Renaissance, against which he rebelled. Frithjof Schuon in fact called him a man of the Middle Ages. Admittedly, Luther rejected scholasticism, of the misuse of which he had much experience. Schuon also called Luther's form of Christianity "a secondary *upâya* amongst other possible *upâyas*".

You quote many *pro domo* Catholic statements, and you make much of Luther's excessive and intemperate language regarding the mass (a violent manner of expression so often found in Catholics,

[1] A full background to the changes made by the Vatican II council and their negative repercussions is provided in Rama Coomaraswamy's book *The Destruction of the Christian Tradition*, published by World Wisdom, Bloomington, Indiana, 2006. (*See also p. 20 in this book.*)

Muslims, Hindus, and Buddhists) in order to bring discredit on his views. Schuon, on the other hand, sees through Luther's language to his meaning, and explains what this is. Protestantism cannot merely be defined as a truncated and deviated Catholicism; truncated it may be, but it is above all a *different* angle of vision (on sacraments and salvation) from that of mainstream Catholicism. In any case, one *upâya* cannot be judged by the criteria of another. I will not attempt to go into this in any detail, as all possible nuances have been exhaustively expounded by Schuon. I therefore earnestly recommend a reading or re-reading of his two articles on Protestantism, which now appear as chapters in two different books.[2]

Protestantism had no causal role with regard to Vatican II. Interestingly enough, the appearance of Protestantism in the 16th century provoked the Council of Trent, in which the ailing Catholic Church put its own house in order, thus enabling it effectively to maintain its witness for a further four centuries. The true predecessors of Vatican II were the Enlightenment, the French Revolution, and the posthumous influence of the nefarious Teilhard de Chardin—not the extremely conservative, anti-democratic, and entirely pre-modern Martin Luther.

*

* *

Regarding the eucharist, I think one can say that it is necessary and that it is not necessary! In saying this, I am thinking of the desert fathers and hermits (male and female) who, for years on end, and by virtue of their own chosen way, had neither the sacrament of penance nor the sacrament of communion. (The invocation of the Holy Name was their eucharist). Towards the end of his life the last traditional Pope, Pius XII, said that the day was coming soon when the faithful would only be able to celebrate the holy sacrifice of the mass on the secret altar of the heart. This could only mean that, *in extremis*, the outward eucharist was dispensable. Literally speaking, he was no doubt referring to those who (because of communism or a falsified church) were materially impeded from celebrating the outward eucharist but, at the same time, his words do indicate the outward "relativity" and "dispensability" of the formal sacrament. I think therefore that his words

[2] "The Question of Evangelicalism" in *Christianity/Islam* and "Christian Divergences" in *In the Face of the Absolute*.

can also be validly applied to those denominations which do not have the Roman mass but have strong faith in the saving power of Christ. Incidentally, a Protestant who is qualified to invoke the Holy Name may, and preferably should, do so in Greek or Latin, for, in invocatory prayer, it is better to use a fixed and hallowed liturgical language, rather than the language of everyday speech.

*

* *

In these days of change, we must cling to the old ways. This is what the word "tradition" means. If we throw away our most precious possessions (those beliefs and practices that have been handed down to us), we have betrayed our trust, and have nothing precious to hand on to *our* successors. In this way, tradition is broken—and we are responsible. The best-loved English hymn says:

> Change and decay in all around I see.
> O Thou who changest not, abide with me.

The two saints for the "modern" age are St. John-Baptist Vianney (the Curé d'Ars) and St. Theresa of Lisieux. They are the beacons for Catholics of our time. They fiercely combated the "modern world" which, in their day, had already begun. May they intercede for us now!

Amongst the great saints of the past, of whom your father used to speak much, were St. Francis of Assisi, St. Bernard of Clairvaux, and St. Thomas Aquinas.

These are the bright stars in our dark firmament.

General

I never cease to recall the four-fold teaching of Frithjof Schuon:

1. Discrimination between the Real and the unreal.
2. Permanent concentration on the Real.
3. The practice of the virtues, especially humility and generosity.
4. A framework of beauty (dwelling, clothes, life-style).

In other words, Truth, Prayer, Virtue, Beauty. Virtue is inward Beauty, and Beauty is outward Virtue.

The first item above is the doorway to the other three, namely, implacable and dispassionate discernment between the solid rock of truth and phantasms of whatever sort is an indispensable prerequisite for any successful endeavor. The first and highest virtue is objectivity; it is the most precious of the Holy Spirit's gifts to man—the antidote for pride and passion, and the key to self-knowledge (i.e. humility). The 20th century Algerian Sheikh Ahmad al-'Alawî said: "Truth melteth like snow in the hands of him whose soul melteth not like snow in the hands of truth." In a similar vein, Christ said: "Ye shall know the truth and the truth shall make you free." The converse is also true: every separation from the truth enslaves us. Objectivity is prior to all else.

*

*   *

There are many different kinds of sanctity. From literature and from our upbringing, we are most familiar with sentimental, emotional, and devotional forms, and we unconsciously judge spiritual matters against this background. But Shakespeare said that there are more things in Heaven and earth than we have ever dreamed of, and Jesus said that in His Father's House there are *many* mansions. There are many forms of spirituality, and the highest may well be described as pure *jñâna* (the way of knowledge or "gnosis"), in other words, the *religio perennis*. Needless to say, this does not preclude Love and Sacrifice. Far from it. The *religio perennis* would be impossible without the love and the fear of God. Nevertheless, the climate of *jñâna* is very different from that of *bhakti*, and it can sometimes be disconcerting for those who do not know what to expect.

*

*   *

Frithjof Schuon's paintings of the Virgin Mary portray, not the historical Virgin, but her heavenly and eternal prototype, namely Mercy, both virginal and maternal, which is identical with the Islamic *Rahma* and the Hindu *Lakshmi*. The formal inspiration of these paintings is strongly Hindu and more or less "shaktic" or "tantric". They must be appreciated according to the criteria of Hindu sensitivity and not according to those of Semitic moralism. The Semitic mind tends to "animalize" sexuality, whereas the Hindu mind tends to "divinize" it. There is a great interiorizing power in these paintings, and this is apparent to those with a contemplative temperament and to those who are prepared for them through an acquaintanceship with Hindu art.

Admittedly, there is in nudity a *de facto* ambiguity because of the passional nature of man; but there is not only passional nature, there is also the gift of contemplativity which can neutralize it, as is precisely the case with sacred nudity amongst traditional people. Likewise, there is not only the seduction of appearances, there is also the metaphysical transparency of phenomena, which permits one to perceive the archetypal essence through visual experience. St. Nonnos, when he beheld St. Pelagia entering the baptismal font naked, praised God for having put into human beauty not only an occasion for fall, but also an occasion for ascent towards God.

*

* *

I accept with joy the words of Jesus which you quote ("pray for your enemies"). One who carried out Jesus' injunction was Pope Pius XII. He prayed for Stalin—but he spent much of his reign attacking "atheistic communism" and defining Stalin as the enemy of Christianity. You can't pray for your enemies unless you know who and what they are! (Alas, most people, *in their private lives*, declare and define their own personal enemies only too well, but they do not accord to others the same "privilege"!)

It has been said that "we must hate the sin and love the sinner". This sounds good, and indeed it may be a partial truth. But unfortunately there is often, if not always, a sort of amalgam between the sin and the sinner, which makes it impossible to hate the former without also hating the latter! Am I being too hard? Well, consider: which one among us loves Hitler? We have to be careful about how we express ourselves. Alas, the only way we can express our "love" for a murderer is by leading him to his due punishment—while saying, as we lead him there, "May the Lord have mercy on your soul"! Jesus was forever talking about hellfire, outer darkness, gnashing of teeth, etc., and about those who, according to his vision, deserved such horrors. In the personal lives of the vast majority of people I have known, I have seen *very little forgiving of one's personal enemies*. On the other hand, almost everyone is a superlative expert at forgiving *other people's* enemies! (It is wonderfully easy, and it gives one a wonderful feeling). This makes me blush. It is *infra dignitatem* to rush to forgive other people's enemies. It is far too easy! Let us rather try to do something difficult: let us try to forgive *our own*. Let me make this clear, by means of an example: it is not for me to forgive Hitler for the holocaust; it is for the Jews to decide whether or not they can forgive him (and I am not saying that they should). If and when the Jews forgive Hitler, then (and only then) will I be in a position to consider forgiving him also.

*

* *

Religion is a *form* of Truth (it is "colored"), and as such it is accessible to the whole community. The "*pure* Truth" ("uncolored") is for the very few. But people don't like to hear about what they disparagingly call "elitism"!

Christ said: "Ye shall know the Truth, and the Truth shall make you free."

Truth never dies, even if it is forgotten and obscured by modern men. Since it never dies, it has representatives and spokesmen in every age. In the modern age, it is found amongst traditional Platonists and traditional Vedantists—not amongst pseudo-Platonists and pseudo-Vedantists. The traditional representatives are very few in number.

Truth is prior to all else. "Truth" (right belief or right thinking) is the first item of the Buddhist Eightfold Path. Doctrine, then method; theory, then practice. For this reason, our doctrine, or our theory, has to be true!

APPENDIX II
Biography of William Stoddart

William Stoddart was born in 1925 in the village of Carstairs in southern Scotland. His early schooling was in that locality, and later he attended the University of Glasgow, where he studied French, German, and Spanish. Since that early start, he has been an enthusiast for the treasures of Western European languages and literatures. Later, still at the same university, he graduated in medicine, with further studies at the universities of Edinburgh and Dublin.

From his early youth, Stoddart was interested in seeking to understand the profound meaning of things. In an interview with Lynn Pollack (2003), he recalled: "I was raised in a simple and elementary Protestantism (the Bible, God, Christ, and prayer). I never rejected these things but, already at the age of twelve, I made the wonderful discovery of the Eastern religions. This was thanks to my father who, as a marine engineer, went frequently to India and worked with Indians, many of whom I met when their ships were in British ports, and also to my early education, which involved receiving elementary information about Hinduism and Islam." He later added: "It never for a moment entered my head that these religions could be false. I knew instinctively that they were true, but had no idea at the time just how much the doctrine of 'the transcendent unity of the religions' was going to mean for me in later life. I should add that this intuition of the validity of the non-Christian religions in no way weakened my attachment to Christianity."

In 1945, at the age of 20, Stoddart discovered the writings of Ananda Coomaraswamy. This decisively changed, and gave direction to, his life. For the first time, he began consciously to understand what was meant by "objectivity" and absolute truth. In one of Coomaraswamy's books, he came across the name of René Guénon and, having sensed that this was someone of significance, he experienced, in 1946, his first encounter with Guénon's works. Of this experience, he said: "I found it difficult to believe that anyone could go so much further than Coomaraswamy, but Guénon certainly did." But there was more—much more—to come. On his first visit to Paris in 1947, he discovered, in a left-bank bookstore, the journal *Études Traditionnelles*, which was the vehicle for Guénon's writings. Stoddart immediately subscribed to this journal, and bought all the back numbers that were available. Again in the above-mentioned interview, he described the sequel to this as follows: "I went through these numbers one by one, systematically reading all the articles by Guénon. Then I looked at the other articles. One evening I noticed an article entitled 'Modes of Spiritual Realization'. It looked as if it were along Guénonian lines, so I plunged into it and, as I slowly made my way through it, I had the experience of a whole 'Taj Mahal' of truth—crystalline and 'symmetrical'—being constructed before my eyes! This article went so much further than René Guénon! Was such a thing possible? It was as if one were being transported bodily into the Kingdom of Heaven! I wondered: 'Who on earth can be the author of such an article?' So I looked for the author's name, and saw 'Frithjof Schuon'. I immediately picked up the whole bundle of *Études Traditionnelles* that was in my possession and looked for everything that this Frithjof Schuon had written. There were only a few items at that time, but fortunately there were some. I eagerly read these, and was totally transported by them."

Stoddart traveled much during his life. Soon after the end of the second world war he began his Continental explorations. In 1947 he visited France and Belgium, in 1949 Spain and Portugal, and in 1950 Italy. On this last trip, he discovered, in a bookshop in Florence, the name and address (in Naples) of an Italian translator and publisher of Schuon's writings, and he there and then decided to proceed to Naples in order to visit him. This was to be his first meeting with someone familiar with the Guénon-Schuon teachings, and this person, in addition to informing him about many things, also gave him the addresses of similarly-minded people in London. Thus began a life-long association with the Guénon-Schuon school of intellectuality and spirituality, a school which in due course became known as the "traditionalist" or "perennialist" school.

Stoddart graduated in medicine in 1949. After a few years in general practice, he became a clinical research physician in the pharmaceutical industry, an occupation in which he spent most of his working life. From 1950 to 1952, he was a medical officer in the British army—military service being compulsory at that time—and was stationed in Hamburg, Germany. This was a linguistic godsend for Stoddart, as it enabled him to deepen his knowledge of the German language, something which, for very specific reasons, was to stand him, later in life, in very good stead.

Stoddart's working life caused him to spend several years firstly in Manchester and then in Glasgow, but during these years he paid frequent visits to his traditionalist friends in London, as well as continuing with his European travels. In 1968, Stoddart moved definitively to London, where he spent the rest of his working life until he retired to Windsor, Ontario, in 1982. More of this later.

Frithjof Schuon resided in Lausanne, Switzerland and, in 1950, Stoddart paid his first visit to Lausanne. There he met many of Schuon's friends, but (as he has said) he was too afraid to ask for an interview with Schuon himself! Only three years later, in 1953, did he return to Lausanne, with the sole object of meeting Frithjof Schuon. This was the first of a life-time of meetings with him, for henceforth Frithjof Schuon was Stoddart's spiritual mentor. From these days onwards Stoddart also enjoyed a close association with Schuon's friend and collaborator Titus Burckhardt.

People often asked Stoddart what Schuon was like, and what he could tell them about him. In an interview with Michael Fitzgerald (2005), he described Schuon as follows: "Schuon was a combination of majesty and humility; of rigor and love. He was made of objectivity and incorruptibility, coupled with compassion. In meeting with him many times during a period of nearly five decades, the immediate personal qualities which constantly struck me were his infinite patience and his infinite generosity."

Mention was made above of Stoddart's love of European languages. Stoddart was enthralled by the 3,500 didactic and aphoristic poems which Schuon wrote during the last few years of his life. Schuon's twenty or more philosophical works were written in French, but his poems were in German, his native language. In collaboration with Schuon and his wife, Stoddart participated in the project of making this vast collection of inspired poems available in English. He also translated into English several of Schuon's French books, and several of Titus Burckhardt's German books.

Stoddart had indeed a life-long interest in languages, ethnicities, and religious cultures. Aristotle said that each language is a "soul", and consequently it can be said that each language is also a "world". Even more importantly, each religion is a "soul", and each religious culture is a "world". Besides being an expression of divine truth, and offering the believer a means of salvation, each religion and, within it, each major "division" or "sector" (but not every minor sect or cult!) has its own perfume or *baraka*. It was with this conviction, and in this spirit, that Stoddart engaged in his many travels, which, in fact, were exercises in religious and cultural assimilation. For example, from the very beginning of his travels in the 1940s and 1950s, he was acutely conscious of, and sensitive to, Western European Catholic civilization as he traveled in the Catholic countries (especially France, Spain, and Italy, but also Ireland and Poland), to 16th century Protestantism as he traveled in Northern Europe (especially Germany, Holland, and Scandinavia), and to Orthodoxy as he traveled in Eastern Europe (specifically to Greece, Russia, and Serbia).

It was not long before Stoddart began visiting non-European religions and countries: Islam (in Morocco, Turkey, and Bosnia); Hinduism (in India); *Hînayâna* Buddhism (in Sri Lanka), and *Mahâyâna* Buddhism and Shinto (in Japan). Indeed—apart from the spiritual life as such—Stoddart's main interest has always been *Religionswissenschaft*, or "comparative religion", as it used to be called. In the light of his readings and travels, Stoddart authored three short books: *Hinduism and its Spiritual Masters*, *Outline of Buddhism*, and *Sufism: The Mystical Doctrines and Methods of Islam.* Each of these was published in several languages besides English. He has also contributed articles to a variety of learned journals throughout the world. For more than four decades, his essays have been appearing in prestigious publications such as *Studies in Comparative Religion* (England), *Sophia* (USA), *Sacred Web* (Canada), *Connaissance des Religions* (France), *Sophia Perennis* (Spain), *Religio Perennis* (Brazil), and *Caminos* (Mexico). For many years Stoddart was also the assistant editor of the British journal *Studies in Comparative Religion.*

Stoddart's books and essays have been acclaimed for their clarity and, in particular, for their "synthetic" or "essentialistic" character. A reviewer in the American journal *Sophia* (4, 2, Winter 1998) wrote: "Stoddart has a tremendous capacity for synthesis; he is in fact a master of synthesis, an author who is able to extract the essence of the phenomena that he examines." In the same vein, Professor Huston Smith expressed his astonishment at how Stoddart, in his relatively short books, managed to compress so much information into such a small compass. The late Annemarie Schimmel, professor of Islamic Studies at Harvard, in reference to Stoddart's book on Sufism, remarked on the clarity of his expression. Montgomery Watt, professor of Islamic studies at Edinburgh University, wrote: "Stoddart's book is no mere academic study, but a presentation of Sufism as one possible way of salvation." Mark Tully, the BBC bureau chief in New Delhi, considered his book on Hinduism to be a unique and remarkable guide.

Reference was made above to Stoddart's frequent meetings with Frithjof Schuon while the latter lived in Lausanne. When, in 1980, Schuon moved to Bloomington, Indiana, Stoddart, like several other of his European followers, decided to follow him to the new world. In 1982, Stoddart moved to Windsor, Ontario, so as to be able to continue his personal relationship with his august spiritual mentor. Stoddart had to choose Canada rather than U.S.A., because it was easier for him to immigrate to the former than to the latter. Windsor is in fact the geographical point in Canada that is closest to Bloomington.

Once resident in Canada, Stoddart remained active in writing, translating, and editing in the field of the philosophy of religion. In addition to his many trips to Bloomington, he continued to make occasional journeys to Europe and Asia. On all his journeyings Stoddart visited and made friends with traditionalists or perennialists in many European countries as well as in India and Japan, and especially with his colleagues and collaborators in Brazil, with whom he formed a close relationship. He also conducts a voluminous correspondence with friends and enquirers all over the world.

In Windsor, Ontario, where he now lives, Stoddart has a simple but charming home, full of interesting books and *objets d'art* from each of the great religious civilizations. The fact that his present abode faces, on the one side, the serene waters of Lake St. Clair and, on the other, the busy Detroit River, evokes the happy combination of deep serenity and prodigious intellectual output that is the characteristic mark of Stoddart's personality.

Mateus Soares de Azevedo

SOURCES

1. "Progress or the *Kali Yuga?*": *Journal of Oriental Research* (Madras, India), special volume, 1973.

2. "Meaning behind the Absurd": Preface to *In Quest of the Sacred*, edited by Seyyed Hossein Nasr and Katherine O'Brien (the proceedings of the Congress of Traditional Studies, Lima, Peru, August 1985). Oakton, VA: Foundation for Traditional Studies, 1994.

3. "Traditional and Modern Civilizations": Based on a lecture delivered at the Fitzwilliam Museum, Cambridge, England, on 17 June 1992; reprinted, in part, in *Sophia* (Newsletter of the Foundation for Traditional Studies, Oakton, VA), December 1992.

4. "Ideological Obstacles to the Spiritual Life": Previously unpublished.

5. "Religious and Ethnic Conflict in the Light of the Writings of the Perennialist School": Lecture delivered at the Department of Religious Studies, University of South Carolina, 1993, entitled "Inter-religious Conflict or 'Communalism' in the Light of the Writings of the Traditionalist or Perennialist school; *Sacred Web 9* (Vancouver, Canada), n.d. (c. 2000).

6. "The Flaws of the Evolutionist Hypothesis": Previously unpublished.

7. "The Flaws of Democracy": Previously unpublished in English.

   Portuguese translation: Introduction to Tage Lindbom, *The Myth of Democracy*. São Paulo: Ibrasa, 2007.

8. "What is Religion?": In *Outline of Buddhism*. Oakton, VA: Foundation for Traditional Studies, 1998.

9. "What is Orthodoxy?": In *Outline of Buddhism*. Oakton, VA: Foundation for Traditional Studies, 1998.

10. "What is the Intellect?": Previously unpublished.

11. "Frithjof Schuon and the Perennialist School": Previously unpublished.

12. "The Role of Culture in Education": *Studies in Comparative Religion* (London), vol. 17, nos. 1 & 2 (n.d. [1986]); *Every Branch in Me: Essays on the Meaning of Man*, edited by Barry McDonald. Bloomington, IN: World Wisdom, 2002.

13. "The Masculine and the Feminine": Previously unpublished.

14. "Mysticism": In *The Unanimous Tradition*, edited by Ranjit Fernando. Colombo, Sri Lanka: Sri Lanka Institute of Traditional Studies, 1991; *Sacred Web 2* (Vancouver, Canada), n.d. (c. 1995); *Ye Shall Know the Truth: Christianity and the Perennial Philosophy*, edited by Mateus Soares de Azevedo. Bloomington, IN: World Wisdom, 2005.

    Spanish translation: "Misticismo", *Caminos* (Guanajuato, Mexico), 2ª epoca, no. 12, Summer 1998.

    Portuguese translation: "Misticismo", *Religio Perennis* (São Paulo, Brazil), vol. 1, no. 2, 1988.

15. "The Role of Obedience in Spirituality": Previously unpublished.

16. "Aspects of Islamic Esoterism" (excerpt): *Studies in Comparative Religion* (London), vol. 13, nos. 3 & 4, Summer-Autumn 1979; *Sufism: Love and Wisdom*, edited by Jean-Louis Michon and Roger Gaetani. Bloomington, IN: World Wisdom, 2006.

    German translation: "Anblicke islamischer Esoterik", *INITIATIVE 42: Wissende, Verschwiegene, Eingeweihte—Hinführung zur Esoterik* [*INITIATIVE 42: Gnostics, Quietists, Initiates—A Guide to Esoterism*]. München: Herderbücherei, 1981.

17. "A Visit to Mount Athos": *Sophia* (Newsletter of the Foundation for Traditional Studies, Oakton, VA), no. 7, Fall, 1994.

18. "A Visit to the Jagadguru": Previously unpublished in English.

    French translation: "Une visite au Jagadguru", *Connaissance des Religions* (Nancy, France), vol. VII, no. 2, 1991.
    Italian translation: "Una Visita al Jagadguru", *Viátor* (Rovereto, Italy), 2004.

19. "The Meaning of Tantra": In Abdul Wahid Radhu, *Islam in Tibet.* Louisville, KY: Fons Vitae, 1997.

    Portuguese translation: "O Tantra no Budismo Tibetano", *Religio Perennis* (São Paulo, Brazil), vol. 1, no. 1, 1977.

GLOSSARY

anamnesis (Greek): "remembrance" or "reminiscence"; the Platonic doctrine that knowledge is a recalling of truths latent in the *Nous* or *Pneuma* ("Intellect" or "Spirit"). "We need not so much to be taught as to be *reminded*" (Samuel Johnson).

apocatastasis (Greek): The final dissolution of the universe; the return of all things to God. This doctrine was expounded by Origen, Clement of Alexandria, St. Gregory of Nyssa, and St. Gregory Nazianzus. *Apocatastasis* corresponds to the Sanskrit term *pralaya*; see *yuga*

baraka (Arabic): spiritual influence, blessing, grace.

castes: the four spiritual temperaments, or social stations, according to Hinduism; see p. 65.

creationism and emanationism: respectively the Semitic and Aryan modes of cosmogony. In the symbolism of the spider's web, creationism looks at the concentric circles, and emanationism looks at the spokes (or rays). Creationism is transcendentist, and emanationism is immanentist. In the writings of St. Thomas Aquinas, it is shown that the two viewpoints are not in conflict, but are compatible.

emanationism: see creationism and emanationism

entropy: the principle that complexity tends towards degradation; that systems naturally move to a greater degree of randomness; the second law of thermodynamics.

esoterism: (1) the correlative of *exoterism*, the latter being the outer form, and the former being the inner essence, of a religion—respectively the "kernel" and the "shell". The outer form, the "exoterism", is for the whole collectivity, and is sufficient for salvation; the inner essence, the "esoterism", is for those who have a vocation for it. St. Paul puts a particularly sharp edge on the matter in his words: "The letter killeth, but the spirit giveth life"; (2) a synonym for the Total Truth, the various exoterisms being so many partial truths. In this sense, *esoterism* is the Uncolored Truth, and the various exoterisms are the refractions—or "colors"—of the Truth.

Filioque (Latin): the term which expresses the theological doctrine that the Holy Spirit proceeds from the Father *and from the Son.* This doctrine was promoted by Western Christians from the 6th century onwards, and officially adopted by the Roman Catholic Church in 1014. It is rejected by the Eastern Orthodox Church, which retains the formulation of the original Creeds, namely, that the Holy Spirit proceeds "from the Father alone".

gnosis (Greek): knowledge. The term "gnosis" is cognate with the Sanskrit *jñâna.* A "gnostic" (a "knower") is one who, by temperament, has a predisposition for gnosis; in Hindu terms, this is the distinction between *jñâna* (knowledge [or discernment]) and *bhakti* (love [or devotion]). A "gnostic" is a *jñânin.* This usage of the terms "gnosis" and "gnostic" is independent of their use in connection with the early Christian heresy of "gnosticism".

initiation: from the Latin *initium,* "beginning". The rite of entry into a religion (e.g., Christian baptism), or into a spiritual path.

Intellect: this term is used to indicate the first element in the ternary "*Pneuma (Nous)-psyche-soma*" (Greek), "*Spiritus (Intellectus)-anima-corpus*" (Latin), or "Spirit (Intellect)-soul-body". In the words of Eckhart: *Aliquid est in anima quod est increatum et increabile. Si tota anima esset talis, esset increatus et increabilis; et hoc est Intellectus.* "There is something in the soul that is uncreated and uncreatable. If all the soul were thus, it would be uncreated and uncreatable; and this is the Intellect." "Intellect" is synonymous with "Spirit", but the former pertains principally to Truth (or doctrine) and the latter principally to Being (or spiritual realization). The adjective "intellectual" (used in the sense here described) is synonymous with the adjectives "gnostic" and "jñânic". See table on p. 78.

metaphysics: this term is used to describe a philosophy which takes into account the distinction between the Divine Essence ("Beyond-Being" or the Supra-Personal God) and "Being" (or the Personal God). It is found *inter alia* in *Vedânta*, Platonism, and the writings of Eckhart and St. Gregory Palamas. This distinction is made clear in the doctrine of the "Five Divine Presences" or "Five Levels of Reality", which are: the

Divine Essence ("Beyond-Being" or the Supra-Personal God), "Being" (or the Personal God), the Intellectual or Angelic Realm ("universal manifestation"), the soul ("subtle manifestation"), and the body or the material world ("gross manifestation"). See table on p. 78.

Nous (Greek), *Intellectus* (Latin): "Intellect" in the Medieval or Scholastic sense; the faculty of gnosis or knowledge; cf. Arabic *'Aql*; see Intellect

philosophy: in the history of philosophy, the three great divisions are: Ancient (or Greek) philosophy; Medieval (or Scholastic) philosophy; and modern philosophy, beginning with Descartes and Kant. As Frithjof Schuon has pointed out, Ancient and Medieval philosophy has its staring point in certainty, whereas modern philosophy has its starting point in doubt.

Sat-Chit-Ânanda [or *saccidânanda*] (Sanskrit): "Being-Consciousness-Bliss" or alternatively "Object-Subject-Union"; an epithet applied to the Divinity, but which is also reflected in cosmology.

Scholasticism: Medieval Catholic philosophy; the most renowned amongst the scholastics was St. Thomas Aquinas, author of the *Summa Theologica.*

yuga (Sanskrit): "age". According to Hindu doctrine, each great temporal cycle consists of four "ages" or *yugas*. These are the *Krita-Yuga*, the *Treta-Yuga*, the *Dvapara-Yuga*, and the *Kali-Yuga*, and they correspond to what Classical Antiquity knew as the Golden Age, the Silver Age, the Bronze Age, and the Iron Age. *Kali-Yuga* means literally "Dark Age", and Hindus aver that we are now in the final phase, the one which precedes the final dissolution of the universe and the return of all things to God (*pralaya* [Sanskrit] or *apocatastasis* [Greek]).

For a glossary of all key foreign words used in books published by World Wisdom, including metaphysical terms in English, consult: www.DictionaryofSpiritualTerms.org.
This on-line Dictionary of Spiritual Terms provides extensive definitions, examples and related terms in other languages.

BIOGRAPHICAL NOTES

MATEUS SOARES DE AZEVEDO is a writer and journalist from Minas Gerais, central Brazil. He studied journalism at the Catholic University of São Paulo, modern languages at the University of São Paulo, and History of Religions and International Relations at George Washington University (USA). He also holds a master's degree in the History of Religions from the University of São Paulo, with a thesis on the relevance of the Perennial Philosophy for contemporary thought. For many years he worked as a journalist in the International Affairs section of major newspapers.

He is the author of five books and more than 50 articles and essays on the importance of traditional religion and spirituality in the contemporary world, several of them translated into English and Spanish. He has contributed articles to journals and magazines in the USA, Canada, Spain, France, and Brazil, including the Perennialist journals *Sacred Web* and *Sophia*. He has also translated, and had published, books by C. S. Lewis, Frithjof Schuon, Martin Lings, and Rama Coomaraswamy into Portuguese. He is the editor of the anthology *Ye Shall Know The Truth: Christianity and the Perennial Philosophy* (World Wisdom, 2005). His latest book is *A Inteligência da Fé: Cristianismo, Islam e Judaismo* (Rio de Janeiro, 2006). Soares de Azevedo visited Frithjof Schuon several times in Bloomington Indiana. He lives with his wife and two children in downtown São Paulo.

ALBERTO VASCONCELLOS QUEIROZ was born and raised in the Brazilian city of Santos, the largest seaport in Latin America. He studied psychology at the Pontifical Catholic University in São Paulo where he graduated as a professional psychologist. After graduating, he moved to the city of São José dos Campos, where he began his career working in industry. He soon turned to the public sector, initially as a psychologist in residential care units, and later as a municipal administrator. He is now an assistant to the Mayor's Office, with special responsibility for educational projects.

Queiroz had an early interest in literature and foreign languages, and is an autodidact in English and French. For several years he worked as a translator, and as a newspaper editor. During his university years, Queiroz discovered the writings of the French philosopher and orientalist René Guénon and the German philosopher and poet Frithjof Schuon, who from then on were to be the main influence in his life. Queiroz traveled several times to the United States to visit Schuon, and has assisted in the translation of his works into Portuguese. He lives with his wife and six children in a beautiful country location not far from São José dos Campos.

SUBJECT INDEX

INDEX OF PEOPLES, PERSONS, AND PLACES

Other Titles in the Perennial Philosophy Series by World Wisdom

A Christian Pilgrim in India: The Spiritual Journey of Swami Abhishiktananda (Henri Le Saux), by Harry Oldmeadow, 2008
The Betrayal of Tradition: Essays on the Spiritual Crisis of Modernity, edited by Harry Oldmeadow, 2005
Borderlands of the Spirit: Reflections on a Sacred Science of Mind, by John Herlihy, 2005
A Buddhist Spectrum: Contributions to Buddhist-Christian Dialogue, by Marco Pallis, 2003
The Essential Ananda K. Coomaraswamy, edited by Rama P. Coomaraswamy, 2004
The Essential Martin Lings, edited by Reza Shah-Kazemi and Emma Clark, 2009
The Essential René Guénon, edited by James Wetmore, 2009
The Essential Seyyed Hossein Nasr, edited by William C. Chittick, 2007
The Essential Sophia, edited by Seyyed Hossein Nasr and Katherine O'Brien, 2006
The Essential Titus Burckhardt: Reflections on Sacred Art, Faiths, and Civilizations, edited by William Stoddart, 2003
Every Branch in Me: Essays on the Meaning of Man, edited by Barry McDonald, 2002
Figures of Speech or Figures of Thought? The Traditional View of Art, by Ananda K. Coomaraswamy, 2007
A Guide to Hindu Spirituality, by Arvind Sharma, 2006
Islam, Fundamentalism, and the Betrayal of Tradition: Essays by Western Muslim Scholars, edited by Joseph E.B. Lumbard, 2004
Journeys East: 20th Century Western Encounters with Eastern Religious Traditions, by Harry Oldmeadow, 2004
Light From the East: Eastern Wisdom for the Modern West, edited by Harry Oldmeadow, 2007
Living in Amida's Universal Vow: Essays in Shin Buddhism, edited by Alfred Bloom, 2004
Of the Land and the Spirit: The Essential Lord Northbourne on Ecology and Religion, edited by Joseph A. Fitzgerald, 2008
Paths to the Heart: Sufism and the Christian East, edited by James S. Cutsinger, 2002

Returning to the Essential: Selected Writings of Jean Biès,
translated by Deborah Weiss-Dutilh, 2004
Science and the Myth of Progress,
edited by Mehrdad M. Zarandi, 2003
Seeing God Everywhere: Essays on Nature and the Sacred,
edited by Barry McDonald, 2003
Singing the Way: Insights in Poetry and Spiritual Transformation,
by Patrick Laude, 2005
The Spiritual Legacy of the North American Indian: Commemorative Edition, by Joseph E. Brown, 2007
Sufism: Love & Wisdom, edited by Jean-Louis Michon and Roger Gaetani, 2006
The Underlying Religion: An Introduction to the Perennial Philosophy, edited by Martin Lings and Clinton Minnaar, 2007
Ye Shall Know the Truth: Christianity and the Perennial Philosophy, edited by Mateus Soares de Azevedo, 2005